AF529164

IMPACT OF INTERNET ON JOURNALISM

IMPACT OF INTERNET ON JOURNALISM

ARUN BHATIA

AKANSHA PUBLISHING HOUSE
NEW DELHI

AKANSHA PUBLISHING HOUSE
R 37-B, Vani Vihar, Uttam Nagar
New Delhi-110059
Email: ektabooks@yahoo.com

Showroom
4649/21B, Ansari Road
Darya Ganj
New Delhi - 110 002
Ph.: 23269193 / 9811582579

Impact of Internet on Journalism

© *Author*
First Edition 2005
ISBN 81-8370-018-7

All rights reserved. Including the right to translate or to reproduce this book or parts thereof except for brief quotations in critical reviews.

[he responsibility for the facts stated, conclusions reached etc. is entirely that of the Author. The publisher is not responsible for them, whatsoever.]

PRINTED IN INDIA

Published by M.P. Misra for Akansha Publishing House, New Delhi and *Printed at* : Mehra Offset Press, New Delhi.

Contents

Preface

The impact of the internet on journalism takes a reflective turn. Not only has the internet changed journalism, it has forced people to rethink different aspects of journalism, journalism practices, journalism education and the way journalists have framed the discussions about this new medium.

The internet promises to have a larger impact on journalism than any of the changes in information and communication technology that have preceded it. Internet has emerged as a viable publishing medium; it offers journalists a new set of reporting skill; it has an impact on readers and the information to which they have access; and it has changed the way people think about issues related to journalism. In short, it is not too much to conclude that the internet has changed, and will continue to change, almost every aspect of journalism.

Computerisation in all sectors of society has taken place in particularly global democracies — with effects on the way the economy and society operates. Practically all media companies have switched to computer network systems, electronic communication traffic and the 'paperless office' are topics of debate in management circles and the convergence of media as well as the fact that the television set, video player and personal computer have found their way into an increasing number of households are signs of the high impact of technology on all aspects of life. The internet as it can be considered to be affecting journalism in general and the professional ideology of journalism in particular.

Although it must be said that every country or region has its own specific issues regarding new media developments and journalism. The internet had a fast start virtually everywhere, although initially there were not many publicly available electronic resources.

This book is an in-depth look at the way journalists used the internet and also have on journalism ethics.

Editor

1

Communication Freedom in the Age of Internet

Regulation of communication in liberal democracies is mainly based on traditional principles of freedom: freedom from state interference, that is to say, no government action to prohibit a publication before it has taken place and, the other side of the coin, the right or freedom to express oneself. Over the years, inmost countries in Western Europe the "freedom to" principle has come to be safeguarded by the state as well:

— governments do have an obligation to enable freedom of expression and
— a diversity of ideas.

The idea of diversity or plurality—as both the result of freedom of expression and a prerequisite for democratic discourse—refers, firstly, to the number and variety of providers of information. Thus state support for ailing newspapers in order to guarantee a certain level of pluralism in the production of information has become a common feature of many a Keynesian welfare state. A concern for pluriformity might also lead governments to stimulate new entrants and thus competition in the telecommunications sector.

Another aspect is the diversity of information contents. It is defined as an obligation of many European public broadcasting corporations which are expected to provide a "reasonable ratio of information, culture, entertainment and education," as stated in the 1967 Broadcasting Law in the Netherlands.

A third and central aspect of the freedom of expression and the plurality of information is the right of access to channels of communication, enabling reflection or representation of the prevailing differences of opinion and culture in a given society. The fundamental conditions for effective access are freedom and opportunity to speak out, and thus a sufficient number of independent and different channels, plus autonomy over media access opportunities. Access to the network for all on equal terms, and a guarantee of continuity of the "universal service" performed by public telecommunications operators are typical examples.

As all these aspects of guaranteeing diversity imply some form of government action—be it prohibiting, prescribing or supporting—based on concrete decisions and an abstract notion of the "general interest," there is by definition an inbuilt tension in the traditional idea of communication freedom. In order to improve the "freedom to," one might well have to be a bit lenient with the "freedom from." And there are other, more legal, limitations to the principle of freedom. To put it bluntly, freedom of the one person or group usually meets its boundary where it interferes with the freedom of the other.

Communication freedom is thus legally limited in most countries by privacy laws, property rights, libel laws, a perceived threat to state security and public order, and some norms of taste and decency. Although we are facing the beginning of a supranational regulation, limitations on communication freedom usually differ from one country to another. Regarding taste and decency, the cultural differences between countries are most clear. What is tolerated or even appreciated in one country might be a sin in another. Especially in the area of "explicit material," countries like the Netherlands and Denmark have a more liberal stand than, the UK or the US.

Information Services

To understand the complexity of different areas and kinds of the existing communication regulations, it is useful to distinguish between different types of information services. According to Bordewijk and Van Kaam, communication patterns may be characterised in terms of two dimensions, i.e., central versus individual control of information storage and central versus individual control of timetable of distribution and choice of subject. The combination of these two dimensions results in four basic communication patterns: allocution, consultation, registration and conversation.

In allocution—one-to- many communication with usually little personal feedback opportunity—information is distributed from a centre that decides the timetable of communication simultaneously to many peripheral receivers. The most common example is broadcasting, where programmes are received by large numbers of scattered individuals at the same time. Consultation refers to a many-toone-to-many situation in which individuals at the periphery look for information at a central storage of information, like a library, database or teletext.

Registration is in effect, the consultation pattern in reverse, in that a centre searches for information from a participant at the periphery; with the centre usually determining the content and occurrence of the communication traffic and often without the awareness of the individual. This many-to-one communication applies to all systems of surveillance and relates to a variety of services: from automatic recording at a central exchange of telephone calls to audience research and for purposes of charging consumers.

In cases of conversation, individuals interact directly with each other, bypassing a centre or intermediary and choosing their partners, time, and topic of communication by themselves. It is a one-to-one pattern of communication, usually with symmetry and balance between the parties, like in an exchange of personal letters or the use of electronic mail.

Another relevant dimension in comparing these different information services or communication patterns is that between the public and private domains, areas where traditionally different fields of regulation apply: privacy and property rights more in the private domain, public order and taste and decency more in the public domain.

Mass media contents, for instance, which are widely available to all without restriction are most public by their nature, while the registration and storage of data concerning people or organisations are least public. Conversation services are more likely than consultation services to belong to the private sphere, although the ostentatious use of portable phones in public places seems to point to a cultural shift.

The allocution pattern, more than the other three, is associated with the "old media" of mass communication. Not that old necessarily means dying in due course - as some say is the case with newspapers. The allocutive pattern remains important and may still grow in absolute amount of traffic. Especially consultation and conversation however, have been able to grow because of new telematics - combining telecommunications, informatics and digitalisation - and the diffusion of video and sound recording equipment. The steady increase of subscription and pay per-view channels, as part of the explosion of cable and satellite television, will further contribute to a relative decline in allocution. At the same time, computerisation and extended telecommunication connections have favoured the growth of registration potential.

Regulatory Domains

New information and communication technologies are said to demonstrate three basic trends: the redistribution of information traffic from allocutary to conversational and consultative patterns; the shift of emphasis from the public to the private domain; and the convergence, overlap and interconnection of communication functions and technologies. In spite of these trends, many national communication systems are still regulated according to their basic technology and often for historic reasons.

Thus, print media are almost entirely free from regulation or control and often protected and privileged, as they are judged to be the prime vehicle for the expression of opinions and the control of decision makers in a democracy. Even with the increase of mergers, take-overs and cross-media ownership, and the threat to diversity it might have, many governments still hesitate to set rules for, and limits to, press concentration. Prohibitive interference in an imperfect market is still seen as a violation of the freedom to publish, a freedom generally regarded as co-extensive with freedom of speech.

The principle of freedom of communication got a somewhat different interpretation when, during the nineteenth century, telegraph and telephone, and later telecommunications became popular. To solve market imperfections, these so-called "common carrier" media were often regulated as to their infrastructure, ownership and pricing, while there was no regulation of contents. They were considered a natural monopoly which should provide universal service. All over Europe, the regulatory regime of cable networks and telecommunication services has recently been shifting towards a press model, with liberalisation of the market and privatisation of the services.

Broadcasting, historically due to the physical scarcity of frequencies, has always been much more subject to regulation. In public broadcasting systems, the scarcity usually meant a semi-monopoly situation, where governments or government controlled bodies decided on who was allowed the entrance, and on what grounds. At the same time, a central collection of license fees had to be organised in order to finance programming. Together with the supposedly intrusive and at the same time distractive nature of the medium television, this prompted governments to set all kinds of norms and standards for entry and performance. Liberalisation and privatisation represent a deregulatory trend in terms of the structure of the broadcasting market; the content, however, remains an area where rules are eminent.

Although there is a hesitant trend towards convergence of these three policy domains, new information and communication technologies go beyond the separate boundaries and, even more so, beyond those of the separate countries. This poses special problems. Does the common carrier element of much ICT ask for regulation of infrastructure and access? Should the press or broadcasting model be applied to the content? Is ICT the new battleground for deciding the "openness" of a society? All questions relate, in one way or the other, to the problem of communication freedom, especially where ICT is applied in the field of political communication, participation and democracy.

ICTs in Politics

One should not forget that many ICT, and the Internet in particular, were first implemented in the area of defence and surveillance. At the moment, they are primarily treasured for their economic potential, and regulation of access and content is hardly a part of the industrial logic. The relative shift in information traffic from allocution to consultation and conversation is also largely a consequence of its economic use.

Most large enterprises in the US and more than half in the Netherlands have a site on the Internet. In taking over the "backbone" of the Internet from the National Science Foundation in 1995, the US telecommunication giants Sprint, American and Pacific Bell were more interested in the commercial than possible democratic opportunities.

American and European publishers and newspapers get "on line" not because this is an extra medium to inform, but because it is a potential market and a means to avoid distribution and paper costs. They are also afraid that others might takeoff with their classified ads and thus with an important part of their income. The technology-push policy of the Dutch government, spending ECU 30 million on infrastructure and the development of consumer services, in order to get one million Dutch on the Internet by 1997, is particularly inspired by the social and economic potential of telematics development in Europe, and the aim to be in its forefront.

For most political decision makers, the applications in political communication have been a spin off from the industrial policy. Not so for the grass roots movements which have hailed the new medium as a means of enriching democracy. Its flat, open and unstructured organisation, its nonhierarchical and potentially bottom-up structure and the possibility to combine allocution, consultation and conversation through interaction is seen as bringing back direct democracy.

Greek city states where all citizens actively participated in political debate and opinion forming, and often were even obliged to fulfil political tasks in rotation. Many centuries later Rousseau, reminding us in passing that participation in Athens was only by male citizens and made possible because they had slaves and thus a lot of spare time, rephrased the idea of direct democracy in that volont, general could only be achieved by all sharing in its formation. What is often forgotten in references to the Contrat Social is that, according to the French philosopher, direct democracy would prosper best in small communities where citizens are relatively independent and the difference between rich and poor is small.

Rousseau's ideas about democracy paved the way for universal suffrage in the 19th and 20th century. But where he saw an obligation for the people to actively participate in politics, the earliest election studies in the US and the UK during the Second World War and shortly after it demonstrated that even voting, the minimal participation in the political process, was not common among all and interest in the political affairs was an exception. While some sawnon-voting as a serious problem in a democracy, modern democratic theorists such as Joseph Schumpeter labelled notions like the "will of the people" and the "general will "a myth. He criticised the classical idea that the final goal of democracy is the emancipation of the dignity and happiness of the individual through significant participation in decision making. Schumpeter proposed instead a democratic "method", an "institutional arrangement for arriving at political decisions in which individuals acquire the power to decide by means of a competitive struggle for the people's vote".

Although representative democracy is often seen as the second best solution, democracy as a method is the political form liberal democracies have taken. All this has led to a call for a return to direct democracy as a favoured cure and ICT, readily available with its communicative possibilities, as its vehicle.

While Internet is renowned for its global reach and lack of frontiers, it is worth noting that the more interesting, democracy related applications and experiments with ICT are taking place at the local level. Several experiments show that the Netherlands, with a cable density of around 85 per cent, a PC in every four out of ten households and in 1995 around 300 thousand people using the Internet, is a European forerunner in interactive political uses of ICT.

The so-called City Talks in Amsterdam were a prudent attempt to combine allocution with conversation and consultation. Based on a limited form of two-way communication, the local municipality initiated from 1989 a series of live discussion programmes on "hot" issues on the local television channel "Salto." Although television is by definition an allocutory, one-way medium, this public access channel has for years facilitated minority groups to voice ideas and broadcast cultural experiments. In the "Talks" politicians and representatives of non-governmental organisations discussed a chosen topic, while the home audience could get extra background information via teletext and react to the opinions voiced. These reactions were then included in the debate, while the viewers could also vote for certain statements or policy options.

The philosophy was "information in reverse:" citizens telling politicians what they think of certain issues instead of politicians gaining support for decisions by explaining and persuading. It was a limited form of input-democracy, with wants and desires articulated and formulated bottom-up. In spite of its open structure, or may be because of it, none of the actors were really happy with the space they got to make their say. The non-politicians were also dissatisfied with the lack of follow-up in terms of political consequences. In 1995 the programme was moved to the local semi-commercial channel AT5 and the interactive element taken out to give it more the format of a talk show.

Consultation services — especially in the area of consumer use—are probably the most publicised where it comes to ICT applications. Electronic banking, teleshopping, electronic bulletin boards, etc. have not yet become common place but are beginning to be part of everyday discourse. D-bases of newspaper archives, of laws, government reports, parliamentary questions and minutes, of libraries, of demographic statistical data, of all kinds of information relevant for opinion forming have become accessible for everyone, and in some cases only for a minimal price. Political parties have begun bullet in boards, where voters can retrieve information. All parties in the Netherlands have e-mail addresses, some have set up a mailing list to which one can subscribe while others have opened up home pages on the World Wide Web.

The way and speed in which data can be retrieved, stored, analysed, manipulated and sent has certainly affected the registration and surveillance potential of civil servants and politicians. Tele-polling and other computer aided techniques have made it possible to use knowledge about public opinion in the policy making process. In an experiment in Rotterdam with two-way cable citizens were electronically questioned about wants and grievances and plans are now drawn up to organise instant referenda and electronic discussions.

It is this development which enables advanced marketing techniques in election campaigns which are often seen as another example of the "Americanisation" of electoral politics in Europe.

Socialising Democracy

The majority of examples to be found about the use of ICT in relation to democracy is usually of an instrumental kind: applications aim at improving the existing representative democracy. In general they are initiated from the top and mostly based on giving more and better access to more information. Only very few of the ICT applications go for a more communicative use, socialising democracy, improving the "responsiveness of political representatives, active citizenship, communication and public debate instead of information, consultation and registration, bottom-up instead of top-down, responsibility shared by decision makers and the public".

With socialisation of democracy, allocution, conversation and consultation are interactively combined. Such is the case with most of the now seven existing so-called Digital Cities in the Netherlands. The first opened in Amsterdam, in January 1994, organised by a group of citizens, actively involved in cultural, political and the hacker's movement. Essentially, this Digital City is a site on the Internet, representing Amsterdam as a virtual city and a virtual community with, for example, a library, coffee bar, post office, museum. The idea is that citizens build there own city, there are streets and squares sharing a certain "sphere," people can "rent" flats and "construct" houses.

The City's philosophy is bottom-up, non-hierarchical and voluntary, and the interface is user-friendly. Discussion groups have started in virtual public spaces on a variety of topics, of which the traditional political issues form however a minority. The emphasis is on horizontal debate between citizens, without intermediaries, and between citizens and politicians and it thus functions as a community network, articulating wants and grievances. Digital City's town hall provides access to the administrative information system, while political parties publish their programmes, policy documents and political stands.

For access one needs a PC and a modem and for full use one has to log in via an Internet provider. Public terminals have been placed in libraries, museums, the townhall and homes for the elderly. Although access is free, the users form a relatively elite group. Digital City claims a population of some 35000 and around 5,000 consultations a day; the majority of the citizens is young, well educated, employed or studying and male.

The issues coming up in discussions about the instrumental or socialising applications of ICT partly overlap with the recent hype around and prohibitive regulations of Internet. In the former the undertone is concern for participation and political consequences, while in the latter the worry is about content and sometimes clouded by a moral panic. But the discussion is also clouded by the fact that the "euphorics" are allergic to the word "regulation," while those in favour refuse to acknowledge that ICT might be a "technology of freedom. "The adherents of the two positions usually talk at different levels and thus fail to see that there is more between heaven and earth than dirty pictures or the interfering state. At the heart is a question about the conditions for and limitations of communication freedom.

Broken down, the issues at stake in the role of ICT in politics seem to be about access, privacy, content, political representation and control of politics: is one to worry about the discrepancy between optimal access and limited participation; does the unregulated structure revive the "old" contradiction between communication freedom and privacy; should norms be enforced for content and who is responsible; and what will be the effect on democratic control with the changing role or even disappearance of the traditional actors in political communication: political parties and journalists?

Access

Access refers, in the first place, to the openness of a network or technology to both information providers and information users. Where in the economic applications there is a growing number of providers, with the political applications ideally the difference between providers and users disappears. With the non-hierarchical, horizontal organisation structure and the interactive possibilities senders become receivers and vice versa.

Secondly, access is operationalised as the physical, affordable, user friendly and reliable opportunity to make use of a channel or network. At the moment access to ICT is usually restricted to either terminals placed in public places or offices which are "on line." It is not surprising that most users enter the Digital City during office hours. If ICT is considered crucial in the realisation of sociopolitical and economic goals in society - and e.g. the Dutch government's subsidy for Internet-use points to that underlying discourse - then it should be considered as a common carrier type "public service," guaranteed by the state and apparent in universal geographical and affordable access, and universal quality and tariffs.

That does not necessarily mean universal use, let alone maximum participation. At the moment ICT is very much for an elite and applications in political communication point to a use by those already able to find their way into the decision making arena. The question is whether a minimum percentage and representativeness is necessary in order to talk about socialisation of democracy through ICT, or whether different levels of participation only point to a more flexible citizenship. Certainly, the situation at the moment is far from direct democracy, but discussions about the lack of representativeness and low participation tend to turn opportunity into obligation: instead of imposing conditions for participation one imposes participation itself.

There is also a problematic assumption in this Athenian style obligation to participate, namely that people are political animals. Apart from consulting government services, most people are seldom involved in politics and rarely searching purposefully and actively for political information. The interactive possibilities of ICT, the sensitivity to new social issues that can derive from the horizontal structure and the issue-orientation of news groups might contribute to more information and involvement in debate, but it runs the risk of a self-defeating prophecy and thus turning the high hopes around ICT into a self-fulfilling disappointment.

The danger is that the potential for participation in debate is enlarged, but that it takes place in a public vacuum: active participation grows but passive participation diminishes. Many news groups on the Internet or in the Digital City drown in the cacophony of their own communications without many people listening or hearing.

Privacy

The freedom of the one might well be the insult of the other, or touching on his freedom. A major boundary of communication freedom is set by privacy, a boundary which is not static but constantly under pressure. Journalists test the privacy of public figures in the tabloid press or through muckraking in investigative reporting. Police and other repressive state apparatuses rock the balance of proportionality between their tracing mandate and their privacy protection responsibility. The surveillance potential of the new technologies in Europe has probably found its apotheosis in the Schengen Information System (SIS). European integration and the opening up of frontiers has led to synchronisation of the respective computer systems of immigration, security and police services in the different EU-countries to control the movements of non-EU-members.

Knowledge from computer aided polls, discussion groups or interactive programmes like the Amsterdam City Talks does give invaluable information to decision makers about people and their wishes. It might well influence the political agenda from below and politicians have to take stock of these opinions. The data from mass and the deduction of profiles from the many d-bases available on demographic data and people's consumer behaviour can, on the other hand, be combined to target specific groups in society with specific information and thus turning "coproduction "into allocution, debate into persuasion again.

The tension between communication freedom and privacy is not always recognised or admitted here. Complaints about the misuse of privacy in the case of the Amsterdam Green Left party and their direct mail campaign to the tennis park protesters were turned down by the Amsterdam municipality. Targeted communication is becoming more and more popular. According to Selnow all presidential candidates inthe 1992 US election applied it and with the advancement of technology in the past four years, the 1996 election campaign will also see a combination of databases, e-mail, direct mail and other forms of targeted campaigns with restricted information.

Content

Is it not a paradox that in telecommunications, the recently most liberalised and privatised domain, prior restraint is being reintroduced by net provider CompuServe with the blocking of access to the Internet of some 200 news groups? The pornographic and in some cases racist content of certain news groups seem to be the most pressing issue in relation to communication freedom and regulation.

The problem with Internet is its cross-frontier character: information "unwelcome" in one country "migrates" to another to find a free area. Originally national prohibitions did not count because Internet does not pay attention to local boundaries. But as long as there is no geographical way of excluding particular news groups, chances are that national regulation catches up with this migration. The most restrictive policy then becomes the dominant one for all, be it sex in Germany or the US, racism in Germany or the Netherlands, and may be in the near future religion, politics, etc. in other countries.

The moral panic over some of the content of the Internet and the call for regulation brings back memories of the introduction of the printing press, newspapers, film, radio and television. Restrictions and often some form of regulation or even censorship of their content have been common place in the first phase of new media. And it was mostly the provider that was held responsible: the printer, publisher, bookshop or bookstand, the telephone or cable company and now the access providerson Internet.

The choice seems to be between a tightly regulated information network where the most restrictive national values of one country are applicable to all or a network the content of which is constantly challenging the limits of free speech in a democracy or of the sexual norms in certain countries. Experimental forms of teledemocracy take place at the local level, but it is the global nature of the Internet that is threatening communication freedom.

Although the US Communications Decency Act and the actions of CompuServe point to a serious tension between theory and practice of free speech in the information society, civil liberties movements tend to idealise the Internet news groups as a sort of vehicles for world direct democracy.

Internet is important for consultation to strengthen democracy, news groups less so for conversation, let alone allocution. Rousseau was right when he said that direct democracy prospers best in small communities where citizens are relatively independent and with little difference between rich and poor.

Political Representation

There is another paradox in the arguments about ICT in politics. Where many applications were enthusiastically greeted by party politicians with a silent hope that interaction, debate and more information would lead to a closing of the gap between citizens and politics and thus to a revitalisation of parliamentary democracy, these same applications are said to result in the end of political parties themselves. It is a notion heard among both euphorics who see this as another proof of the directed democratic potential of ICT, and party politicians who suddenly fear they fetched in the Trojan horse. Electronic referenda and other forms of direct contact between decisionmakers and the electorate would render the intermediary function of political parties obsolete.

The arguments of both are flawed, or at least one-sided. Where political parties are traditionally the brokers and articulators of what the wants and grievances in a society are and the translators of these into political demands, news groups on the Internet and discussion groups inthe Digital City tend to strengthen single-issue politics. Moreover, their voluntary nature are not only their strength but also their weakness: no one is committed to the outcome. Debate in news groups might lead to consensus over certain issues, but as long as passive participation diminishes they are not much more than the traditional soapbox allowing for screaming in the dark.

Improvement of consultation potential will make government and administration more transparent and probably more responsive to questions asked. It will remain the function of political parties and elected representatives to make choices between the different particular interests on the basis of a notion of the general interest. That does not mean that these choices should take place in an ivory tower. More than before, the existence of interactive media will mean that listening to and participating in debates -and thus making oneself accountable - becomes a part of the political trade. And politicians could feel a bit uncomfortable with that, as they are more used to persuasiveness than responsiveness. The pallbearers of the political parties forget three more things.

Firstly, that political parties are a recruitment base for future decision makers and power holders, and thus will remain needed.

Secondly, for news groups and discussion platforms to take over the role of intermediary organisations people will have to be come political animals. As we have seen, most of them are not even consumers of political information, let alone political actors. The anarchistic structure of Internet and the open, non-hierarchical structure of initiatives like the DigitalCity can, however, be an incentive for participation.

Thirdly, political parties are needed as the organised control over power holders as, with electronic polling etc. they might base their decisions more on political marketing than ideologies and weighing different interests.

The other controllers of power holders are the media, the watchdogs of democratic politics. Here again the argument goes that their role becomes less important now that people can consult all kinds of sources themselves. Citizens are not dependent anymore on the journalistic selection criteria based on sensational news values, databases are open for them and not only for journalists.

And again this assumption is based on a notion of the public actively and consciously searching for information. In reality political communicationas well as communication use have traditionally been allocutive; over the years we have been allocutively socialised. The noted trend from allocution to more consultation and conversation is first of all a relative one and secondly more the result of industrial use. With the commercialisation of television, the popularity of video as a time shifting apparatus and remote control enabling to "zap" around informative television programmes, political communication becomes more than ever: politicians in search of an audience.

And moreover, with the abundance of information, political marketing and targeted political communication, the critical and selective role of journalism is probably more needed than ever. Discussion and news groups can contribute to debate and opinion forming, but with their non- compelling nature they run the risk of remaining in the discursive public sphere, while journalism can lift issues more easily into the decision making sphere and on the political agenda.

With the same ease that notions like tele-democracy have been introduced, when new information and communication technology was applied in the domain of politics, one now talks of censorship and a return to the dark ages. A German prosecutor, CompuServe and the US government have certainly triggered a debate over communication freedom in the age of Internet. Internet, with the characteristics of telecommunications and the free speech claim of the press, has triggered a kind of regulation which may turn out to be more strict than most broadcasting laws in Western Europe.

Access and content rules with regard to broadcasting were legitimised with the argument of scarcity of channels and the supposedly intrusive nature of the medium. Neither can really be applicable to Internet and other interactive ICT applications. There is an abundance of channels and potentially wide access while the elite character of the users can withstand intrusiveness, if that is the case. Only the position of children is comparable, but it remains a question whether this is a responsibility of the state or of their guardians. The panic, both over the content and regulation of Internet, overshadows the fact that a notion of tele-democracy can really only be used at local applications of ICT, and even than with reluctance. More than content, questions of access and participation, of privacy and registration, of control and representation come here to the fore.

Internet and Information Control: The case of China

Computer-mediated communication (CMC) is ushering in

a new era in the history of mass communication in terms of information and culture transmission across formerly closed or restricted national borders. As more and more countries link their computer networks to the Internet, CMC is quickly expanding both the international and domestic public spheres, through which, according to Habermas, the dissident view is registered, public opinion is formed and eventually rational choice and/or agreement can be made among private individuals.

Although the corporate and technocratic promises of Computopia societies based on the full potential of human creativity and participatory democracies are debatable, advantages of these technologies in breaking through traditional controls of information are apparent. Just as the invention of printing technology made mass communication more of a reality and led to intensified efforts by authoritarian rulers to control information, the development of the world-wide computer networks today poses new challenges to governments in exercising control over the dissemination of information. It is true that CMC has yet to turn itself into a new form of public sphere, considering its difficulty to meet the requirement that all citizens be allowed to participate with low entry cost and with equal access to information. Its potential in expanding the existing public sphere by giving greater freedom to the public in breaking through state domination of and market pressures on mass communication to air and access dissident views should not be underestimated. If "democratic communications are the basis of any democratic culture and political system", we should also expect changes in communications brought about by new technologies to affect a country's culture and political systems.

As the history of mass communication has shown, the most fundamental conflict in communication often takes place between the outlook of the established authorities and media demands for unrestricted freedom of expression. The history of mass communication, in this sense, has evolved around conflicts between the government and media.

New communication technologies, providing greater public space and new ways to break through information controls, often lead to new rounds of conflict. Thus, new technologies often play a vital role in readjusting the balance between the established authorities on the one hand and the public and media on the other. Along the line of such an argument, this study examined the potential impact of CMC on government controls of information in China — one of the few remaining communist countries in the world — where the authorities still want to decide what their people should say and hear by keeping a rigid control over the mass media.

Although "the economic and technological revolution promoted by Deng Xiaoping since 1978 has stripped away much of the ideological prison in which the Chinese had lived for three decades", the Chinese Communist Party and government have never considered giving up their ideological control over the Chinese people. Although leaders of China today are more willing to relax their control for the sake of the country's economic development, they nevertheless are determined not to "sacrifice spiritual civilisation in order to realise and develop the socialist market economy".

CMC Development in China

Computer networks have had a relatively short but momentous history of development, which can be traced to ARPANET, founded in the United States in 1969 to connect universities, the military and defence contractors. Most people date the true arrival of the Internet at 1983, when the National Science Foundation began a networking program to link its six supercomputer centres to the scientific community with Transmission Control Protocol/ Internet Protocol (TCP/IP). This marked the start of what we know today as the Internet, which is actually "an internet work of many networks all running the TCP/IP protocol suite ... connected through gateways and sharing common names and address spaces". The pace of the Internet's growth in the 1990s is spectacular, spreading faster than both cellular phones and fax machines. In June 1991, there were only 130,000 people using the Internet, but the number soon rose to over 8 million in May 1993 and is expected to exceed 100 million in 1998. In early 1995, there were about 33 million Internet users in more than 100 countries.

The advantages of having a country connected to the Internet are obvious. Scientific, financial, business, industrial, military, political and cultural information will all be within easy reach. As the world enters into the Information Age, it has become more and more evident that information is power, whether in political, military or economic terms. Therefore, it is not surprising that China, which has been engaged in unprecedented efforts to overhaulthe national economy, is so anxious to upgrade its infrastructure for information exchange.

China's computer information industry is currently averaging an increase of 28 per cent annually, worth 20 billion US dollars at the end of this century. To date, more than two million computers are being used in offices, management enterprises as well as families all over China; more than 800 databanks have been set up; and there are well over 60,000 enterprises in the information industry. According to a calculation released by Microsoft Corp., China is already the seventh largest personal computer market in the world and it is estimated that it would overtakc France in 1996.

China, as a large nation, appeared rather late on the Internet map for technical reasons. Although some Chinese computer networks established e-mail links to the Internet as early as the late 1980s, computer centres in the country remained internationally isolated until 1994 when several major computer networks began to establish direct links with the Internet. In May 1994, Institute of High Energy Physics (IHEP), a computer network run by the Institute of High Energy Physics of the Chinese Academy of Sciences (CAS) was connected to the Internet through a 64K bps line leased from AT&T. Then in July 1994, IHEP changed its satellite link to submarine link via KEK, the National Laboratory for High Energy Physics in Tsukuba, Japan, to Esnet in the United States. The IHEP link was quickly followed by other links.

The National Computing & Networking Facilities of China (NCFC), which began in 1989 as the first high speed network project funded by a grant from China's State Planning Commission and a World Bank loan, was connected to the NSFNET by a 64K bps satellite link via Sprint International router. NCFC, which embraces the Chinese Academy of Sciences Net (CAS) Peking University Net (PUnet) and Tsinghua University Net (TUnet), also received the country-level domain name ".CN".

Other Chinese computer networks with an Internet link includes Beijing University of Chemical Technology (BUCT), a network operated by the China Education and Research Network (CERNET), a network managed by China's State Education Commission and consisting of ten key universities in China; NJNET, the network of Nanjing which is the first city computer network in China; and ChinaPac and CHINADNN, two government-run commercial networks. With major Chinese computer networks connected to the Internet, paths are paved for Internet access by end users of lower-level or independent networks throughout the country.

At present, eight Internet providers are in place, including the government-funded ChinaNet; China InternetCorp. (CIC), a commercial enterprise; and the China

Education and Research Network (CERNET). By July 1995, the number of computers in China linked to the Internet stood at 6,000 with about 40,000 users. By the end of 1995, the Internet service were expected to accommodate 10,000 computers and 100,000 users. In general, China's Internetted computer networks can be classified into three types: academic, educational and commercial. Computer networks for academic purposes are headed by ChinaNet with NCFC as its backbone, which embraces:

— CAS net (Chinese Academy of Science Network),
— PUnet (Peking University Network),
— TUnet (Tsinghua University Network),
— CAnet (Chinese Academic Network),
— CRNet (China Research Network),
— IHEPnet (Institute of High Energy Physics of CAS),
— SSTC (State Science and Technology Commission network),
— CERNet (Chinese Ecosystem Research Network),
— USTCnet (University of Science & Technology of China campus network),
— NFCwan (National Flood Control wide area network),
— MEFnet (China National Research Centre for Marine Environment Forecast),
— BSTISnet (Beijing Science & Technology Information Society),
— IMnet (Institute of Microbiology of CAS),
— Shanghai Regional Network and Wuhan Regional Network

China Education and Research Network (CERNET), which opened its Internet link via NCFC, is China's first nationwide education and research computer network. The network, which is still under development, will eventually connect all the universities and institutes in China in the near future, as well as secondary and elementary schools and other education and research entities by the end of this century. It currently consists of a national computer network centre, eight regionalnes work centres and a few university campus networks. In addition to the academic and educational computer networks already in place, the Chinese government also began an ambitious plan for a nation-wide digital data network despite little demand for computer information exchange systems from the public sector at present.

New Challenges Posed by CMC

Technologies affect of human life even though their invention may originally target only at changing ways of doing things. This is especially true for information technologies, which often result in changes which are never part of the intention of their inventors. Among things said about the development of new information technologies, there is a popular vision of the average citizen empowered by computer technology, able to communicate honestly and directly, challenging established power and planning political actions that advance democracy. Ever since the Communist Party came to power in 1949, it has successfully used its control of the mass media as the bottle neck to manipulate information flow in and out of the country. Mass media, tamed by the government through direct control and punishment against erring journalists, see themselves as "eyes, ears and the mouthpiece" of the Communist Party.

Remarkable progress has been made in the freedom of press in China since the start of its modern reforms in 1995 The market forces, the increasing public demand for information access and the Communist Party's promise to have a more open government, have brought about unprecedented changes in the Chinese media. These changes can be demonstrated by the Party's recognition of the media's roles in providing information and entertainment, open discussion of press freedom and the media's supervision of the Party and the government. Despite all these welcome changes, the question of freedom of information and of the press remains the "Achilles' heel" of the regime's commitment to the Marxist doctrine.

Freedom of information and of the press, as Party general secretary Jiang Zemin noted, is merely a slogan used by "bourgeois liberals" to battle against the Party and people. The Party's determination to continue its information control was clearly stated in a circular issued by its Central Committee: Newspapers and journals of the Party, radio and television broadcasting stations of the state as well as other relevant publications are mouth piece of the Party and people. They must unconditionally propagate the guidelines, policies and regulations of the Party and government under the leadership of the Party.

The unrest of 1989, which started with student protests, led the Party to reaffirm its control by drafting various policies and regulations against unwanted information and replacing untrustworthy journalists. There newed fervour for a market economy following DengXiaoping's endorsement for further reform in 1992 has forced the Party and government to give more leeway to the media in running their business, but the Party's control of the nation's information flow through monitoring the media, has never been seriously challenged. The media still remains the most important tool for the Party to manipulate public opinion for support.

In addition to exercising tight control of the domestic media, the Chinese government also has tried to ensure the ideological purity of its people by cutting them off from any possible contact with undesirable information. For along time after the Communists took power in China, foreign publications and broadcast programs, except for a limited number approved by the government, were banned in China. At the height of the cultural revolution, people possessing banned publications or listening to "enemy stations, "including Radio Moscow and Taiwan radio stations, were prosecuted as counter-revolutionaries. As a result, China was isolated not only politically and economically but also in terms of information access during that period.

Although such prosecution has virtually come to a stop since the end of the Cultural Revolution, the government ban against importing foreign publications without its approval and on-and-off interference of hostile foreign broadcast have continued. Overseas publications are imported only for use by foreign diplomats, business people and tourists or for restricted circulation among academics and government officials. Foreign television and radio broadcasts are allowed only in hotels for foreign tourists.

In general, however, the focus on information control has shifted more and more from the liability of Chinese citizens to stay away from foreign publications and broadcast to the responsibility of government to stop the inflow of such publications and broadcast programs. At the same time, the government has shown an increasingly more tolerant attitude in this regard. With such a background in mind, it is not difficult to see the potential threats the Internet may pose to the Chinese government in information control.

What the Chinese netters are able to get over the Internet is more than scientific and financial information. The wide connections enjoyed by the Internet make it an ideal electronic forum for diversified exchange of opinions and information. Numerous newsletters, journals, complete volumes of books, pictures, video and audio records are stored and exchanged over the net. Surfing various World Wide Web sites, one can find virtually anything he wants or does not want.

The Chinese government may have been successful in preventing the Chinese media from publishing or broadcasting anything it considers opposing the Chinese Constitution; harming the socialist system and national security; promoting subversion, rebellion, riots and ethnic animosity; and instigating defiance to the leadership of the Communist Party, but Chinese netters could easily be deluged by such materials once they log onto the Internet. With access to the Internet, Chinese netters could easily receive the information from China News Digest or other publications on the Internet, defeating the government's purpose of censorship.

Chinese political dissidents, a large of number of whom were driven out of China by the government to keep the Chinese from hearing from them, have long been trying to influence China's domestic politics, but have so far made little impact on China's politics because of the censoring of information about their activities abroad by the Chinese media. What better means could they have for their propaganda than the Internet? In addition to its own dissidents, the Chinese government will also feel nervous about letting Chinese netters play audience to various political advocates, ranging from communist- haters and human-rightists to proponents for the independence of Tibet or Taiwan. The pornographic materials available on the Internet will also abort all its efforts against the "yellow" culture.

What is more important is that the interactivity and ease of distribution of CMC via the Internet has blurred the distinction between the receiver and publisher of information. Unlike the traditional mass media, where the gatekeeper decides who can publish, the CMC over the Internet allows all netters the right and power to publish without prior censorship, bringing the practice of free expression and free press to an unprecedented scale. Such a unique feature of CMC may not matter much to countries which believe in a free press, but it will prove to be detrimental to the Chinese government's control over information. Though experienced in playing the censor, the Chinese government will find it extremely difficult, if not totally impossible, to control what is being exchanged over the Internet because today's new information technologies defycensorship for a number of reasons.

First, unlike its domestic media, the sources of undesirable information are simply beyond the reach of the Chinese government. Most publishers and senders of such information operate in countries which practice an entirely different type of freedom of speech or of the press and are beyond the jurisdiction of the Chinese government.

Second, the development of computer technologies has greatly accelerated the speed of transferring electronic information and diversified its means of delivery. The mobile nature of information on the Internet makes "detrimental" information, as one expert put it, a "moving target". Even for Chinese netters, the government will find it hard to gather evidence against any involvement in sending or receiving such detrimental information without monitoring all information exchanges, which are too fast and too numerous for careful scrutiny.

Third, new technologies straddle the border between being a mass or interpersonal medium with a convergence on its mail function, information retrieval function, message posting function and broadcasting function. An interpersonal exchange of information could easily result in a massive broadcast. Without a clear distinction made between these two types of communication, law enforcement is impossible without intruding on privacy and other personal rights.

Fourth, in the computer culture magnified by the Internet, maximum freedom is celebrated. The cyberspace culture prescribes free speech and free flow of ideas as the route to social and intellectual progress. The Internet lacks a central controlling body without whose co-operationany attempt of control by the ruler of a single domain are useless. Although managers of the Chinese domain may trycensorship by closing the access of its netters to certainsites as the Chinese networks are doing to the majority of news groups, this does not prevent users from bypassing the local service provider and accessing such censored information via an overseas service provider through telnet, FTP or Gopher functions.

Fifth, the Internet's fault-proof set up resists censorship. A technical blockup is read by the Internet as "damage," which will be say as an error and elicit automatic correction. Dynamic re-routing ensures that if one communication link is broken, the traffic can be redirected through other existing links. The Internet, after all, was designed for military use, and the design criteria expect fault tolerance and reliability even after a nuclear attack.

Sixth, the global interconnectivity in the Information Age complicates an individual country's efforts for law enforcement. In general, it is difficult to enforce criminal laws outside of one's country under international law. It would be difficult to pinpoint the origin of offending information. Even if the origin can be identified, it is still difficult to stop the inflow of such information without effective control over the flow of information from the originating country. Corresponding laws and their enforcement need to be in place in the originating country as well in order for the receiving country to carry out law enforcement or extradition arrangements. This means that censorship by an individual country is almost impossible as long as there are no global standards for censorship.

Despite all the potential problems the Internet connection would bring to China's political and social systems, the Chinese government is nevertheless determined to link the country to the global computer network. By a rough estimate, China still lags behind the world in advanced electronic techniques by 15 to 20 years. A delay in linking up the country with the global computer network would only further enlarge such a gap. While eager to link China's computer networks with the Internet, the Chinese government has never wavered in its determination to maintain its control over information and extend its censorship policy to communication over the Internet. As Chinese Minister of Posts and Telecommunication, Wu Jichuan, said "by linking with the Internet, we don't mean absolute freedom of information. "He explained that China would adopt "management measures" to make sure that only acceptable information gets through to its people. A participant of the Chinese Ministry of Posts and Telecommunication at a meeting of the Internet Society in Hawaii in June 1995 also revealed that China was planning to block access to objectionable information.

Although specific regulations regarding the use of Internet are yet to be announced, existing regulations regarding computer information systems can apply to the Internet services too. The Regulations on Safeguarding Computer Information Systems issued by the Chinese government in February 1994 could be cited as an example. Although the regulations focus on protecting computer information systems and classified information, several provisions can easily be applied to Internet users. Among other things, the regulations provide in Article 7 that "no organisation or individual may use computer information systems to engage in activities that endanger national or collective interests, as well as the legitimate interests of citizens." Such an all-embracing rule can cover all the Chinese netters.

In addition, Article 12 stipulates that "individuals who ship, bring, or mail computer information media into or out of the country shall file truthful declarations with the customs authorities." Such a rule will affect all Chinese netters who wish to download electronic publications over the Internet and even those who send or receive personal electronic mail messages, though whether reading such publications over the net should be considered bringing them into the country is debatable. Much will be subject to the deliberation of the authority in charge. What will perhaps prove to be most scary for the Chinese netters is that the regulations put the authority of enforcement of the rules into the hands of the public security and state security organs, with which no Chinese in their right mind wants to get involved.

Another set of regulations that may affect Chinese netters is that on electronic publications. According to a directive from China's Press and Publications Administration (PPA), electronic publications must be produced by approved publishing houses with an assigned book number, or imported with authorisation by the PPA before they can bedistributed, sold, or rented on the market. Starting on April 1, 1995, all new and reprinted electronic publications must bear an assigned standard Chinese book number of six digits. Although these regulations may not directly affecton-line materials yet, the government official who announced the directive was quoted as saying "we will certainly regulate on-line publications in the future".

Another means for the government to ensure censorship lies in its control over Internet service providers in the same way as it controls the mass media in China. Computer network operators work as censors and gatekeepers in the same way as journalists do by keeping certain information out of the reach of Chinese netters, despite the fact that such censorship could be technically by-passed anyway. The China Internet Corp., China's largest commercial Internet service provider, announced recently that the company's network will bar any "smut, politics or decadent Western culture. By eliminating these things not related to business, we will make better use of the Internet, as resources will be at a lower cost."

The government-run ChinaNet is also censoring information that traverses its access lines according to Wu Jichuan, Minister of Post and Telecommunications, who noted that "as a sovereign state, China will exercise control over this information". In addition, Chinese netters are also warned for "proper use" of the net by service providers. For example, the State Information Centre warns users of its network in the application form that they will be held responsible for inaccurate and illegal information posted on the net. There is enough evidence to show that such tactics do work in China where the Internet surfers are either technically not sophisticated enough to bypass censors or afraid to do so.

Realising the technical impossibility of completely censoring all undesirable information over the Internet, the government also employs the most traditional means of censorship - limiting the public access, by granting such access only to people who not only need to use the Internet for government-approved purposes but are also politically reliable and manageable. When e-mail link was first established between the Internet and China's computer networks, access was granted only to a few hundred of the country's top scientists and researchers. When the Internet becomes more accessible with direct links established between the global computer network and China's various computer systems, priority is given to staff of academic institutions and government offices.

The reason for such control is simple - government and academic institutions are more controllable than private companies and institutions. The effectiveness of such a measure could be seen in a case involving the computer network of the IHEP, a pioneer in China's Internet connection. From April to June 1994, a few IHEP users received e-mail messages discussing the 1989 crackdown of the Chinese student protest and issues related to the independence of Taiwan and Tibet. Officials of the institute were so nervous that they immediately reported the "incident" to higher authorities, and took the occasion to reiterate the policy against the use of computer systems for illegal purposes.

Although public access to the Internet is officially approved and opened in April 1995, the actual number of independent users of the Internet service remains small. By the end of 1995, there were only about 10,000 Internet users in China. Of the 4,000 users of China Internet, which is the most attractive to individual users because of its free installation and low user fees, only 45 per cent are individual users. On the one hand, the high user fees, which could easily run into a few hundred yuàn a month, keep the service out of the reach of ordinary Chinese citizens.

On the otherhand, the state monopoly on providing Internet service limits the on-line access. Requests to get leased lines from the government to make the Internet access more available to the general public have been shelved by government officials even though such requests are mainly for legitimate research purposes. What is ironic is that in June 1995, two months after the Internet service was opened to the public, the Chinese Ministry of Posts and Telecommunications issued new regulations to restrict public access and use of the Internet in light of increasing undesirable access from inside China to political news and information via the Internet by means of electronic mail, FTP, Gopher, World Wide Web, Usenet and so on.

There is further indication that the Chinese government is ready to crack down on the unrestricted exchange of information over the net. Only eight months after China officially opened public access to the Internet, the Communist Party and the State Council, China's cabinet, issued a circular in December 1995, ordering the service providers to take measures to stop "pornographic and detrimental information" from entering the country via the Internet

On January 1,1996, Internet service providers were told that new subscription to their service must be postponed indefinitely and no additional permit would be granted to establish international links. Three weeks later, it was announced that the State Council, China's cabinet, approved a set of draft regulations on access to the international computer network designed to strengthen controls over on-line links with the outside world. The new regulations are expected to be made law by the State Council for implementation after some "revisions".

Implications

A paradoxical praxis of the 20th century communism lies in its political unreformability despite its acknowledged need for economic reforms. The question of freedom of information and of the press will remain a taboo in China as long as the government does not give up its commitment to the Marxist doctrine. Since the political system itself depends on the manipulation of information for survival, it is impossible for the Chinese government to give a free re into the Internet penetration in China. In its quest for modernisation, the Chinese government had no choice but to let the country join the global computer networking. Such a decision was a result of the government's desire to catch up with the advanced countries in scientific and economic development rather than a change in its stand on information control to ensure the continued leadership of the Communist Party.

Unfortunately for the Chinese government, however, the development of new information technologies has reached such a stage that these technologies make it difficult to maintain the existing level of censorship. Although determined to not let the Internet access destroy the equilibrium of the Communist society, the Chinese authorities are yet to fully realise the potential threat of the Internet to the country's political system. As Microsoft Corp.

President Bill Gates said that Chinese officials might not understand that to implement full Internet access and maintain censorship, they would almost have to have someone looking over the shoulder of every user. The strategies and tactics that have been traditionally used by the Chinese government in controlling the mass media are critically challenged by the Internetted CMC.

There is already a sense of freedom among Chinese netters. Unlike the traditional media, for which the government plays the role of censor and gatekeeper, the Internet provides an efficient and safe forum for Chinese users to discuss politically sensitive issues and exchange information censored by the government- controlled media.

A few years ago, a person would have been in real trouble if found talking by phone to blacklisted overseas activists". As a result, the new communication revolution is likely to affect the way information is generated, distributed and consumed in China. The fact that the Internet allows more open-ended access to outside information and creates dynamic interaction between the media and audience, poses a direct challenge to the Communist Party's control over the communication channels and contributes to the transformation of China's existing communication system.

In the face of the potential explosion of all kinds of information, both desired and undesired, that could come as a result of the Internet connection, the Chinese governmentfinds it hard to locate the bottleneck for information control in the cyberspace. At present, it has no choice but to slow down the process of plunging the country into the cyberspace by drafting new laws and regulations, controlling the Internet service providers and limiting public access until it can find a right balance between control and access.

Such actions, however, defeat the very purpose of connecting China to the global information network because it also hampers the flow of desirable information in and out of the country. All signs seem to indicate that the Chinese government is determined not to let the Internet connection destroy its controls over what the Chinese people should hear and see, to say less about what they want to say and show. At the same time, Chinese leaders also seem genuinely concerned about the possibility that China would further lag behind in scientific and economic development if it is left out of the cyberspace.

While it cannot be denied that the Internet connection will greatly challenge the Chinese government's control of information and media, it must be acknowledged that the Internet connection is unlikely to produce fundamental changes in China's political system or media system in the foreseeable future. On the one hand, the environment fordrastic political changes in China is no longer present. The government high-handed policy towards political dissent and the lures of the market economy have made the Chinese people less politically active and more materialistic than they were in 1989. On the other hand, the role of the Internet in promoting the public sphere for the Chinese society is limited by at least two factors.

First, access to the Internet is unequally distributed due to government restrictions as well as its high cost and technical know-how required. As a result, the Internet is mainly used by government officials, scientists and businessmen mainly for financial and scientific purposes. The number of net users in China no doubt will rise dramatically by the end of this century, but it will take much longer before CMC is able to pass from its current elite stage to the mass stage. Without massive participation in the electronic communication over the net, it is impossible for CMC to replace the government controlled mass media as a major source of information despite its advantages in freedom of information and free exchange of ideas.

Second, the fact that communication over the net is mainly conducted in the English language because of the Western dominance also keeps out a large number of potential Chinese users and limits the role that Chinese users could play in the international exchange of information. Although more and more Chinese can communicate in English today, the number of those who can effectively use the language to communicate over the net is still limited. At the same time, net communication in the Chinese language is not as convenient and restricts net activities to communication among China's netters themselves or with Chinese living overseas.

Because of the elite nature of net communication in China, CMC is unlikely to produce any fundamental changes in China's political and communication systems in the near future although it will help to expand and diversify the country's communication structures. In addition, the Internet access may also further enlarge the gap between the Information rich and information poor in the country. With the elite having greater access to information and thus bigger profile in the public sphere, it may make it even more difficult to achieve the goal of participatory democracy on a massive scale.

2

Internet Applications in Print Media

As traditional journalism continues to embrace electronic communication, so too must journalism education. Yet just as journalists struggle to define exactly how electronic media such as the Internet can assist in the research, production and packaging of news and information, so to are journalism schools struggling to incorporate the Internet into traditional courses in reporting, writing and editing. Indeed, many programs are making impressive strides in this endeavor thanks to both available funding and a philosophical recognition by journalism faculty that, yes, online technology is changing the profession in a way journalism education cannot ignore.

In US, at Northwestern University in Evanston, Ill., the Medill School of Journalism is successfully integrating the World Wide Web into its teaching programs. Admittedly, Medill's progress in this area is due in no small part to the nature of Northwestern University's rich technological culture. Northwestern is one of perhaps a half-dozen universities across the nation that has made an absolute and sustained commitment to technology on its campus. The 14,000 undergraduate and graduate students and 1,800 full-time faculty members throughout the university have extensive access to hardware and online tools, including student e-mail accounts which are assigned upon registration, space on servers to create individual websites, and wide access to multiple LEXIS/NEXIS, Dialog and other online database services. In these ways and more, Medill is blessed with the university's overarching commitment and generosity when it comes to technology. It is a blessing that extends itself to the students and, ultimately, the greater journalism profession.

The application of the World Wide Web in journalism education is perhaps most pronounced in Medill's heralded graduate Magazine Publishing Project, the premier professional-training course of its kind in the nation in which the students produce both a prototype magazine and a business plan. As the capstone course in Medill's magazine sequence, the Publishing Project goes beyond traditional journalism classes and focuses on the publishing process in its entirety, including the crucial interrelationships between the editorial, circulation and advertising dimensions of the enterprise. Of particular importance to the development of both research and conceptualizing skills, the class employs the start-up methodology, rather than have the students simply produce an additional issue of an existing publication.

Twice a year at Medill, a class team of 18 graduate students have 12 weeks, or one academic quarter, to conceive, staff, design and produce an original magazine concept, a four-color prototype issue and fully realized five-year business plan. The magazine itself is a professional student-produced editorial product, complete with both departmental pieces and feature articles designed by students using QuarkXpress. The end-result is a 48-page prototype, as well as a number of line extension and ancillary products. Approximately 2,500 copies of the magazine are printed and distributed to Medill alumni, students, faculty and friends and to a large number of prominent editors and publishers in the magazine profession.

The business plan projections are derived from "real-world" testing. These include elements such as the results of actually performed market research, an actually mailed circulation test, and a telephone advertising sales campaign directed at the 250 advertising prospects that received Project media kits.

The core objective of the program is to emulate the complete magazine publishing experience. It is an attempt, from concept to delivery, to mirror the professional realities wherever possible. To that end, each member of the class assumes a traditional staff role-editor, business manager, advertising sales associate-and contributes accordingly over the course of the Project. In that same vein, the hardware and software the Publishing Project uses are chosen with the intent of duplicating the most widely applied industry tools.

Each year, Medill's faculty actively calculations publishing companies throughout the country to assess what applications and computer systems our students need to be fluent in-or at the very least familiar with-in order to enter the job market fully equipped. In 1994, concluded that the majority of magazine publishing companies were in the process of switching to Apple Power Macintosh platforms which, we believe, have since become the industry standard.

Since so much actual magazine reporting, writing and designing in the industry takes place in the QuarkXpress environment, the widespread preference for the Macintosh operating system is certainly understandable. In response, the Magazine Publishing Project has a dedicated classroom equipped with 18 Power Macs as well as several high-end design computers. Each computer has unlimited access to the World Wide Web, and students require little encouragement to dive in and surf. Similar to our hardware selection, our software of choice for Web browsing software also is the current publishing industry standard, Netscape 2.01. As of this writing, we have no plans for replacing

Netscape in favor of other options such as Microsoft's Explorer software, but that, like so much in the world of technology, may change.

Understandably, the Project is an intense process, as students try to accomplish in 12 weeks what often takes most start-up publications one or two years. Students work eleven or more hours a day, often six days a week over the 12-week period. It follows that, given such a brief time, there is every incentive to provide and use labor-saving technology. As a result, the Web fits into the program out of necessity as well as on a need-to-know basis.

With each Publishing Project class, the Web proves an ever-more-valuable resource for both the business and editorial aspects of the Project. In preparing the business plan, the Web provides instrumental research capabilities that help students locate potential advertising prospects, prospective subscribers for the magazine and, for the detailed contents of the five-year business plan, the names and numbers of providers of a variety of publishing services.

The Web's other major contribution to the Project is on the editorial side. In addition to their staff responsibilities, students are required to propose, research and write a departmental piece and a feature article for the Project magazine. The Web plays a valuable role in this respect, and students browse websites for data and sources in all the ways today's working journalists are learning to do. Likewise, the issues students encounter when conducting Web research reflect the legal and ethical issues facing journalism, most critically the accuracy of the information that resides on the Web.

In a way, Medill's faculty is in a somewhat precarious position-advising in the uncharted territory of Web research. Students can be over-eager in their adoption of the Web as a journalistic source; the speed and quantity of information available with a few keystrokes is indeed appealing. The faculty finds itself curiously shading and positioning its guidance to students, simultaneously encouraging use of electronic tools such as the Web while reminding students to maintain the healthy skepticism that is the backbone of fine reporting, regardless of the medium or the source.

Although each student produces two written pieces, not all of them appear in the final printed prototype version of the Project magazine. This dilemma-surely all students involved with the Project should have an opportunity to showcase their work-has also been somewhat solved by the Web. As of Fall 1995, each magazine created by the Publishing Project has a companion, student-developed website. Today, all student work is published on the website, where space limitations are less restricting than a print product.

When Medill originally introduced the website into the Project, it posed a prickly question that soon answered itself. In short, the faculty was concerned with just how to teach Web publishing. Professors debated whether to offer classes in the use of PageMill or Front Page or raw HTML, the coding language of Web-page design. Yet it soon became clear that, in the case of the Publishing Project, students embrace the Web so willingly that they often come to the Project knowing more than faculty.

Many students voluntarily establish their own websites where they post resumes and writing samples-a tremendous advantage during the job search as students often tell interviewers to simply point and click to access their credentials. For students unfamiliar with the Web, they arrive at the Project believing they will learn it by osmosis from their classmates, and they are usually correct. In effect, they teach themselves, so little formal training during the Project is required, although the faculty attempts to make it available at the students' request.

The result is a somewhat free-form, self-administered learning environment, with many faculty tangentially involved but none dedicated solely to Web instruction. At times, this proved to be a very effective pedagogical format; at others, less so.

Despite student enthusiasm for online work, the website component of the Project is another burden for them to shoulder in the very limited time frame of the course. It is, however, a burden most believe worth bearing. Without doubt, developing a website is an ideal opportunity to learn by doing, which is particularly important considering that no true industry standard for Web publishing exists. Students are faced with the same problems all magazine editors and publishers are currently trying to solve.

Nevertheless, the students do spend much effort insuring that the online version of their Project magazine both parallels and complements the print product. This takes a number of forms. For example, prior to any actual design or coding work, the "New Media" team composes a specific vision statement for the website which not only mirrors the vision statement previously created for the magazine as a whole, but also outlines those areas where the online product will be mindful of the medium's unique advantages.

Additionally, a conscious attempt is made not to ghetto-ize the new media effort by isolating it from the rest of the class. Instead, an organizational task-force structure of multiple roles for every member of the class makes it possible to allow some of the students who are designing and editing the print version to be part of the Web team, thus insuring a certain degree of continuity between the two products. With the cumulative experience of four Project websites, a number of interesting thematic issues have arisen which may illuminate a few broader pedagogical considerations. These include:

a) *Strategic positioning issues:* The heart of the matter concerns the core appropriateness of a Web version of any particular magazine. Every magazine prototype class must ask itself a difficult question: Does this particular readership's interest in this particular topic lend itself for Web dissemination? Where are the technological thresholds, and are they sufficiently surpassed? In the case of Today's Smart Parent, for example, the market practice conducted by the students showed that two thirds of families who make up the magazine's potential readership own computers, and that almost half of them are already using the Internet-from which one might reasonably conclude that a Web version of the magazine was a viable idea. Moreover, as the managing editor of the TSP home page aptly noted: "The website was a natural extension to our print magazine concept, because it fit in so well with our vision statement-parents should know how to use all the tools available to improve their children's education and to learn themselves."

b) *Design considerations:* The issue here does not seem to be technologically driven; that is, it is less a matter of software choices and more a matter of aesthetics. Given the wide range of presentation possibilities available with all Web-coding software, the issue of design appropriateness is of ongoing importance. Rather than stipulate a certain design genre, however, perhaps the best guidance to be given to the students is simply to require that sufficient time be spent by everyone concerned browsing the Web, with particular attention focused on the websites of competitive publications.

c) *Editorial procedures*: From our experience, it is clear that the editorial processes and procedures used on a Web version of a magazine are indistinguishable from those employed on print products. These include matters such as copy-flow routines and procedures, fact-checking, assignment and supervision of both "idea" and "line" editing of manuscripts, final copy-editing, and issues of editorial management and decision-making. Hence, the website offers an additional pedagogical opportunity for both core editorial instruction and practical application. Indeed, it has always been apparent that website creation is largely an editorial-driven, rather than technologically driven, venture. In our experience, at the start of the process less technically adept students informally but effectively learn Web production coding from those with greater technical expertise, and once they are sufficiently trained, their roles as online editorial decision-makers become paramount. One unique c onsideration, however, that we encounter is derived from the fact that the printed 48-page prototype does not have room for all the departments and features which the students propose and write. As a result, in the interest of insuring that every student completes the course with at least one "clip" for job interviewing purposes, priority for inclusion on the Project website goes to those articles which-for reasons of editorial balance, not merit-are not included in the printed prototype. However, with no "space" limitations on the website, in the end the online version of the magazines also include some articles which also appear in print.

d) *Building on the past:* When Web versions of our printed prototypes were first contemplated two or three years ago, it was our expectation that each successive Project would consciously build and expand on the work of its predecessors. This has not proven to be the case.

As one might imagine, Medill's students and faculty engage in endless discussions about these and related issues, and admittedly it is a challenging process. Yet by addressing the questions inherent to online journalism, students often enter the work force understanding more about it than seasoned publishing professionals. In this way, the Project once again mirrors the industry, and students are that much more valuable to employers.

Employment opportunities cannot be overstated in a discussion of integrating the Internet into journalism education. Students come to professional education, specifically journalism school at the graduate level, to secure jobs. Undeniably, online jobs in journalism are a growing, albeit new, market niche. Gerald M. Kosicki of Ohio State University and Lee Becker of the University of Georgia, for the 1994-1995 academic year, less than a dozen out of approximately 2,400 journalism student respondents reported they had online jobs.

Yet it was just after that graduating class that the online "wave," as it were, hit the beach, and Web-related career opportunities became far more apparent in the job market once dominated by print and broadcast. Indeed, the Kosicki-Becker calculations for 1995-1996 shows a marked increase in online job interest and potential. In this most recent calcuations, 147 respondents reported seeking online jobs, while 71 actually received online job offers, typically at average salaries $3,000 to $5,000 above the prevailing medians.

The experience at Medill is that between 10 and 20 percent of our most recent graduates secured jobs in new media, working online for publications or in positions with a serious online component. Starting salaries for graduate students in new media jobs range from $30,000 to $40,000, compared to the $25,000 to $35,000 range typical of traditional print positions. These figures suggest just how eager publishing companies are to hire people with experience and a facility for online work. They are perhaps also indicative of where the industry is going and where journalism education must follow. It is quite possible, for instance, that within the next five years Medill's publishing course will produce a paperless magazine. The publication will never be delivered to the printer, but rather be an online product.

All of which seems to be leading to a decidedly unvicious circle: Better salaries and positions leading to more interest on the part of better students leading to better applicants leading to more offers at better salaries. And it is clearly something to which journalism education must respond. But beyond the vocational aspirations and professional hire-ability of our students, there is a larger, perhaps more important dynamic at play here.

Online, the space an article occupies is virtually unlimited, but it's important to understand where human limitations come into play. Online, we can add links and sounds and animation. Online, readers can choose precisely what they want to read and what they want to ignore; they can send e-mail. In light of the well-reported salary premiums, students with Web experience in school will find a growing market for their skills. There are, however, other issues of concern that they foresee having to deal with.

Granted, there remain some students-indeed, there are many journalists—who are hesitant to enter the online arena. They question the journalistic integrity of online publishing, particularly at a time when accepted standards of style, content and ethics are noticeably absent. Indeed, this is a critical discussion, and one of the central roles of journalism educators will be to attempt to ensure that the new electronic media are not abused but rather held to the highest principles. But the undeniable reality remains: "The industry blinked, and the publishing world changed. Today's journalism students are a technologically savvy generation, comfortable with new media and all its potential. That alone has significant implications for the future of journalism and, thus, of journalism education."

Internet-based Magazines

In magazines across the country, journalists have dubbed 1995 as "the year of the Internet." Two reasons explain this designation: the tremendous increase in the number of individuals accessing the Internet and the increasing size of the Internet itself. It is unknown exactly how many people regularly "surf" the 'net, the slang phrase for the Internet.

The complement to the increased number of users has been the growth of the Internet itself. Slow growth had characterized the 'net prior to 1995. In August 1993, there were only 23 World Wide Web sites; a year later there was 3,000. But 1995 witnessed unparalleled growth. Between January and June 1995, the number of Web sites increased six fold-to an estimated 30,000. By January 1996, that number exceeded 70,000.

In tracking the Internet trends, magazine journalists have focused on a number of questions that the 'net posed to society. Stories have focused on a range of issues: from questions about obscenity-"cybersmut" or "cyberporn"—to security concerns and opportunities for advertising and commercial growth and investment. Journalists have also speculated about a new breed of information provider as well as new means of delivering information. At least one of those "new means" of delivering information is the "'zine," Internet-based magazines with the potential to converge audio, video, graphic and print technologies into one product.

This section will look at the content of 'zines, Internet-based magazines, and the individuals who "publish" them to ascertain if, indeed, a "new breed" of information provider is developing and to determine the general subject matter and technological approach of 'zines on the Web. Because the Internet is a relatively recent development, scholarly examination has been limited. Much of the research has focused on the educational ramifications of the Internet. Those studies emphasized the need to acquaint students with the Internet, the need to teach them new search strategies to effectively utilize the information on the 'net, and the ramifications of using this network in the educational system.

Another body of scholarly literature has focused on the legal ramifications of the Internet. The best known- and the most widely cited and criticized-was by Marty Rimm who looked at the amount of pornography on the Internet. The researcher and his team downloaded all available pornographic images from five popular Usenet boards over a four-month period.

Within the Communication discipline, scholarly literature has taken three distinct approaches: focusing on marketing/advertising issues; looking at interactive media and their place in media development, and examining computer networking from an international perspective. The emphasized the need to keep marketing principles in mind as corporations move to the Internet. The concept of target audience was an especially important in the user-driven Internet.

The Internet allows for a certain amount of interactivity in home pages and on-line magazines. E.H. Woodward looked at interactive media in his examination of media development and concluded that interactive media will be to twenty-first century society what television is to the current time. By far the greatest amount of scholarly examination has looked at how computer networks such as Internet will affect other countries. These studies-often provided in scholarly journals of other countries-offered interesting perspectives on Internet's effect on other cultures. Such studies have looked at computer network usage in China, Canada and Australia.

Little academic research has been done on on-line 'zines or magazines. In contrast, specialized business publications catering to the advertising and magazine field, as well as popular magazines, have looked at the on-line magazines, variously termed 'zines, "webzines," "digizines" or just plain "magazines." While many of these stories deal with news events-well-known magazines going on-line or new services being offered, other features have looked at new trends developing and even touched on the ramifications of those developments. Newsweek's special section dealing with "The Year of the Internet" was a case in point.

The dealt with a wide range of issues; but one of the most provocative deal with the "The Net 50," individuals-some of them on-line publishers-who were "computerdom's hottest visionaries." Few of these individuals were associated with current publishing companies. Other in-depth stories focused on magazine publishers who were committing large amounts of money to their on-line sites.

The investment seemed merited in light of new studies that suggested that the development of the Internet, CD-ROM and on-line services may represent a threat to traditional magazine publishing. That conclusion, however, was not necessarily shared by those in the publishing field, who contended that print magazines will continue even as on-line magazines multiply. Indeed, print magazines and newspapers were expected to increase the numbers of on-line magazines. These conflicting accounts along with the assertions of the development of a new group of on-line information provide has led to this study which attempts to provide a base-line examination of on-line magazines.

The World Wide Web is constantly evolving. The number of Web sites increase daily; also increasing is the number of on-line magazines. How the Web looks one day will be different from how it looks the next. Given the dynamic quality of the Web, sampling for this research project became problematic. A number of search engines could have been used to locate and sample currently published Web-based magazines.

The researchers opted to use Yahoo for several reasons. First, Yahoo is the most frequently updated of the directories. Thus, the sample would include not only Web magazines "published" by corporations but also the personal forms of journalism-'zines-that tend to have a shorter life span. Second, Yahoo is easy to use. With its word search options and its categorization by topic, Yahoo represented an ideal vehicle for drawing such a sample.

In addition, coders made notes with regard to the subject of the web site as well as any distinguishing characteristics. It was hoped that this anecdotal evidence would complement the statistical findings. Researchers attempted to access all sampled sites. In a number of instances, the site had been taken off the server or denied the researcher access.

The coders examined 502 on-line magazines from all over the world. However, the greatest number of the magazines where the location was known (N=182, or 63 percent) were produced by U.S. individuals, corporations or educational institutions. The largest number of these sites were located in the Far West, most commonly California. New York state was also a popular home for these on-line magazines. Computer technology and the modem have made geographical location less important. Accordingly, on-line magazines are located throughout the United States. They are, however, least likely to be found in the Plains states (N=6) and Rocky Mountain states.

Although the U.S. clearly dominates in the number of on-line magazines, other countries also have a Web-zine presence. The largest number of these are produced by British individuals, corporations or institutions. The Canadians produced nine of the sampled 'zines. The greatest numbers of the other magazines were produced in industrialized European countries. A few African, Asian and South American countries were also the homes of magazines on the Web. The greatest number of the sampled on-line magazines carried a ".com" extension, which indicated the commercial nature of the web server. The ".net" extension was the second most common, followed by ".edu".

A commercial designation does not necessarily mean permanence on the Web, however. Publishing on-line is as precarious as publishing in the print magazine industry. Almost 14 percent of the magazines sampled were no longer on the server at the time of the coding. Most carried a "404" designation, or a "file not found" notation. A few were more specific in their explanations. On-line magazines published in countries other than the United States faced the greatest likelihood of being discontinued. A U.S. commercial address did not necessarily assure permanence; 40 commercial magazines had either been discontinued or denied access to the coders.

The greatest number of these on-line magazines were edited by men, and written by men for a primarily male audience. Indeed women have little of a distinct editorial presence on these magazines. Few were editors and women produced the greatest amount of editorial material on only 22 on-line magazines. This can only be partially explained by the audiences of these on-line magazines. A large portion of these periodicals were aimed at a male-only audience. However, coders also found that the greatest number of periodicals sampled were aimed at both male and female readers. Only 28 publications have a distinctly female audience, according to coders.

In general categories, who are currently publishing on-line "'zines"? Is this the sample population that produces print magazines? The largest single group producing on-line 'zines were publishers of print magazines. Slightly more than 30 percent of all the sampled 'zines were produced by publishers of print magazines. Most of those sampled sites were the electronic counterparts of a single print product. Thus, PM Zone was the electronic counterpart of Popular

Mechanics; Computer Shopper On-Line was the Web-based version of Computer Shopper print edition; and Communication Arts had both a digital and print version.

The second largest single group publishing 'zines were special interest groups. The third largest 'zines was computer hardware, software or service providers; frequently these were web servers. Publishers of sexually explicit materials represented only a minority of the on-line magazines sampled (4.2 percent).

What are the topics covered in these magazines? The sampled 'zines covered a wide range of topics. Not surprisingly, the largest single group were on-line computer periodicals that were designed to appeal to a consumer audience; 69 of the on-line periodicals dealt with this topic. The second largest group fell within what could be described as a "specialized business" category, or publications designed to cover a specific industry, business or profession; 46 of the sampled 'zines were classified in that manner.

The largest number of that group provided job-related information for those involved in the scientific industries, a broad group that included computer programming, manufacturing and repair. Music 'zines accounted for the greatest number of the "entertainment" publications sampled. The largest number of music 'zines cover "alternative" forms of magazine.

What is the purpose of these 'zines: sales, entertainment, persuasion, personal journalism, other? As might be expected, the greatest number of the 'zines are designed to provide entertainment and information, just as most print magazines do. Just over 50 percent of those sampled existed for that reason. However, providing entertainment and information was not always the reason for these on-line periodicals.

Almost 10 percent of the 'zines sampled were created

to sell products only-these provided no editorial material except descriptions of merchandise offered. The most common product offered in this matter related to computers or computer services. Smaller groups had different purposes. Just over 5 percent of the sampled 'zines were forms of personal journalism, an individual communicating his opinions on a variety of topics. Persuasion was the intent of another 24 'zines.

These were produced primarily by special interest groups and political parties. Another 41 'zines had a purpose which would be categorized as "other." The largest portion of these were print magazine publishers whose only aim in their on-line presence was to sell subscriptions or advertising. They provided no editorial material.

Like print magazines, the greatest portion of the advertising was placed by corporations not affiliated with the 'zine. The greatest number of the advertisers were in some way related to the computer industry. The second largest group of 'zines were publications that carried the advertising of the corporation that also produced the 'zine. This is particularly the case for 'zines produced by companies that are in some way related to the computer and commercial magazine publishers.

General Characteristics

On-line magazines shared a number of characteristics with their print counterparts. Like their sisters in print, 'zines seemed to face an unsure future. The surprisingly high number of "404" or "file not found" notations indicated that there was great instability within this field. This does not differ so greatly from the print magazine industry. The locations of these on-line magazines, likewise, have much in common with their print counterparts. The magazine industry-whether digital or print-is a geographically diffused area.

The staffing of these on-line magazines appeared to differ from practices within the print magazine industry. Published research has indicated that women on print magazines do not necessarily hold the top editorial positions but do often hold many of the writer and sub-editor positions. Findings in this study on on-line magazines suggested that this may not be the case. Women have very little of a distinct editorial presence. Few are editors; few produce the greatest amount of the editorial material.

This is even more disturbing because the greatest number of the on-line periodicals were aimed at both men and women. It is unclear why this is occurring. Researchers in the field have emphasized that design and production of information and communication technologies have been male functions. However, research into the magazine industry has uncovered no "gender gap" in computer technology implementation among editors. Certainly, this situation bears closer examination in future studies.

As noted, print magazine publishers produce only a minority of the on-line 'zines. However, this does not necessarily mean that these publishers use this new medium to its fullest potential. The greatest number of 'zines produced by these publishers were nothing more than promotions for the print product. At the site, browsers are invited to subscribe to or advertise in the print magazine. Often, these sites did offer limited editorial material but this was likely to be nothing more than reprints of features that have been published in the printed magazine.

Thus, the medium's potential for instantaneous updates, search opportunities as well as media convergence was underutilized. As a group the consumer print magazines covering computer topics tended to be the most effective in their 'zines. Many offered frequent updates, search options and innovative linking to sites within of the publishing house. These sites also tended to carry advertising, again an acknowledgment of the potential of this medium.

Although print magazine publishers represented the largest, albeit still a minority. presence among the 'zines, there appears to exist a new kind of "information provider." Actually, there appears to be a number of different new "information providers." However, the "information provider" with the ties to the computer industry merited separate consideration.

The largest number of these publishers were not the big, well known hardware or software corporations like IBM, Microsoft, Adobe or Apple; instead, they were small entrepreneurs that offered web-server opportunities and/ or design and marketing services. Their on-line magazines allowed the creators to showcase their talents, cover favorite topics, and advertise their products.

Bringing in large numbers of readers and expanding the advertising base were not necessarily the motives behind publishing these 'zines. Certainly, more research is needed into this new kind of "information provider." Similarly additional research is needed on the large numbers of special interest groups who are turning to on-line magazines to carry their message into the electronic world. The large number of special interest groups, some of whom have never had a magazine presence, are turning to the web to reach out to others with similar sympathies. A closer examination of these special interest groups is needed.

This research project imposed subject matter classifications from the print magazine industry onto the on-line magazine field. These worked reasonably well. The specialized-business 'zines did fit comfortably into the commonly accepted categories in that field. However, the categorization for the consumer portion of these periodicals-by far the largest number of these 'zines—needs to be fine-tuned to make comparisons between print magazines and on-line periodicals realistic.

Purposes of the 'Zines

'Zines have a wider variety of aims than just simply providing information/ entertainment. Many are little more than catalogs offering products; a number have no commercial base at all and offer personal perspectives only. Others desire to persuade the browser about a point of view. Each of these suggested that more is needed on the purposes of these periodicals themselves.

On-line magazines appeared to be in their infancy with regard to advertising. In this regard, publishers of print magazines appeared to be at an advantage. Experienced in working with advertisers, supplied with media kits and documentation needed to sell advertising, and able to offer "packages,"these publishers are at an advantage in developing this medium's advertising base. And that is exactly what they are beginning to do.

The advertising base has not been similarly utilized by the so-called "new information provider." Not necessarily experienced in soliciting advertising, these new publishers may not yet be ready to craft a commercial base to their creative venture. Certainly, more research is needed into this field. More research is also needed on the advertisers who have chosen to commit to this new medium.

Convergence of Technology

Although the Internet theoretically allows for a convergence of technologies, few on-line magazines have taken advantage of that potential. Those that do use audio and/ or video tend to cover subjects that specifically lend themselves to these media. Obviously, the convergence of audio and video posed technological challenges to these 'zines. Although Internet theoretically can converge, audio, video, animation with the more common print and graphics, the technology is just developing to allow this to happen.

Audio and video files are large and require an enormous amount of download time, even on the fastest 33.6 kb/s modems. The innovation of "real audio," the most common means of provide audio on today's on-line magazines today, makes this more likely since such a file can be used with Netscape and the common 28.8 kb/s modems with negligible download time but only marginal quality. Currently, video on the Web is, at best, grainy. Java, an authoring language, seems to hold the best prospect for adding animation. Until the technological problems are resolved, the promise of the convergence of technology on Internet-based magazines is only a dream.

The statistics illustrate that magazines that contain sexually explicit materials represent only a minority. Nonetheless, some discussion should be made with regard to those sites. Almost all the sites carrying sexually explicit materials wore a kind of "brown paper wrapping." A sedate first screen-typically without nudity-advises the browser that the material contained in the site is adult in content. Before the browser can access the site, he/she must select an option indicating the browser is an adult and is freely entering the site.

Almost all these sites were aimed at heterosexual men. The staple of these sites were photographs of women in various stages of undress. Typically, the photographs are accompanied by biographies, similar in content, detail and tone to Playboy's centerfold descriptions. Women have a certain "girl-next-door" quality. They are secretaries, receptionists and college students, who are interested in making their men "happy."

There were a certain number of key issues and make some comparisons between the digital and the print magazines. It also attempted to point to areas that needed further development and examination. A few general conclusions need to be made. First, on-line magazines represent an exciting new field with tremendous potential. They have the potential to reach a world-wide audience, the potential to converge technologies, the potential for enormous creativity. But the word is "potential." They still face software, hardware, network shortcomings. The graphics-heavy 'zines take forever to load with today's modems. The converging technologies still are at a rudimentary stage. Software and authoring languages still present problems.

Second, the editorial product is uneven. A number of these magazines are graphic masterpieces with little editorial substance. Some are editorially interesting but graphically unappealing. Few have been able to balance graphic and editorial excellence. Some of this may relate to the publishers.

Experienced publishers represent only a minority of this field. The new "information provider" is the majority-whether they are special interest groups, computer-based companies or individuals producing their own 'zines.

Third, as interesting and intriguing as this new medium is, it is not going to replace the print magazine or take over the printed version's advertising base now. Currently, print magazines have built in advantages. The print product is portable. It's easier and more fun to read a slick, glossy magazine in a comfortable chair, away from the computer. It's easier to locate an interesting new magazine on the newsstand than to search the Internet for it. As an artifact, a print magazine probably has a longer life than a print-out of an on-line magazine. But, in the long-run, the on-line 'zine has many advantages over its print sister.

First, on-line magazines have an economic advantage. The costly steps of printing and distribution have been eliminated. These on-line 'zines need not be printed, trimmed, bound and sent through the mails to subscribers. Although a presence on the web is not typically free, web-server expenses are no where near as large as the four-color printing process. Distribution expenses are also less on-line. Search engines provide the names and addresses of on-line 'zines when the browser provides the appropriate terms. Links also represent another excellent way for readers to find the 'zines.

From the advertiser's perspective, the print magazine has the longer life. However, this is not necessarily the case since more and more 'zines are archiving their previous issues on the web. The biggest problem appears to be the resistance of advertisers to venture into this new medium and the inability of many 'zine publishers to provide audience research and the "circulation" information that the advertisers have come to expect.

However, this does not necessarily mean that in the future that these on-line magazines will not represent a competitive threat to print periodicals. This is a new type of information delivery that is just developing. It has tremendous potential that needs to be developed. Today, it is a "site" to be "'zine"; tomorrow it may be the magazine with the "net" profits.

3

Online Newspapers

The Net (both the World Wide Web and the Internet) is fundamentally a tool to allow people around the globe to communicate with each other. Because the Net transcends space and to some degree time, many consider the opportunity to interact simultaneously with multiple people who have related interests if not similar positions or attitudes (e.g., political election web sites that draw visitors/ members from multiple political parties) to be a superior forum to its available alternatives—e.g., call-in talk-radio shows, ham or CB radio conversations, and other methods of "connecting" without traveling.

Until the early 1990s, the Internet was simply a network of computers used to transmit government data and enable academic research and conversations. With the advent of the World Wide Web and online subscription service providers such as America On Line (AOL), CompuServe and Prodigy, Internet traffic began its exponential upswing. In 1998, worldwide Internet users approached 147 million. This is up from only 36 million in 1997 and a mere 19 million in 1996. The CommerceNet/ Nielsen Media survey in June 1998 finds that Internet users over the age of 16 in the United States and Canada grew to 79 million from 58 million at the end of 1997. Although in many areas people still do not have telephones, much less network servers, and for people of low socioeconomic status the costs of computer technology and service access are prohibitive, the evidence suggests that competition and growth are driving costs down and mass usage of the Net is becoming a possibility, particularly in areas of the world with sufficient technological infrastructure.

Online communication is viewed by many as nothing short of revolutionary. It is an opportunity to communicate, learn, share, buy and sell, and perhaps most importantly, to build community in virtual space. Newspapers, as key vehicles for the development of community in modern society, have been extraordinarily interested in the notion of building virtual communities as they move their operations online. By using published reports, original interviews and data from an in-depth case study of a major metropolitan newspaper, this essay examines how online newspapers attempt to create virtual communities on the Net. Only a few years ago, the Net was still being described as a "democratic cyberplace." It was user controlled, highly interactive, and essentially egalitarian. These characteristics fueled the belief that a newsgroup, or these new things called "home pages," could be maintained by a college freshman and be as interesting and attractive as similar sites controlled by larger institutions.

Furthermore, the lack of face-to-face interactions meant that the distribution of power in online conversations might be equalized by not really knowing the gender, race, educational background, etc., of the individuals involved. A cyber-persona was judged by its ideas, not wealth or prestige. Individuals often zoomed about the Net using clever pseudonyms reminiscent of CB "handles" as they participated in various mini-communities in virtual space. Currently, the changes taking place on the Internet and the World Wide Web have radically reoriented our image of the Net both conceptually and ideologically. There is growing concern with the superficial, yet technologically daunting changes brought by the Web.

Some people began to speak louder than others. The egalitarian free-for-all of the pre-Web was now being replaced by a series of pulpits. Those with the programming know-how--not necessarily those with better ideas--took the spotlight. Worse, an elitist technological jargon took over; for example, on the more "advanced" sites, your received a condescending message that advised you to upgrade if you wanted to view the blinking text and rotating globes that the site's sponsor was kind enough to provide for your entertainment. In 1993, Rheingold expressed his concern about "big power and big money." He believed that the Net was still out of the control of the elite but that it might not stay that way for long since big power and big money always found ways to control new communications media when they emerged in the past. As each day passes, the Web becomes more institutionally and commercially driven and it resembles less that egalitarian cyberspace of recent memory than it does a tacky, crowded-with-billboards freeway exit just before any major tourist destination in the U.S.

The Web is now home to an almost unimaginable variety of information, put there by individuals, large companies or organizations, and governments. Online service providers and the Web can be viewed as literally thousands and soon millions of vertical markets of products and services (targeted to specific customer groups) as well as virtual shopping malls and online catalogues. In a culture fiercely resistant to paying for content, some groups are now charging visitors to their sites to post messages. When the Internet became a phenomenon and use spread beyond the government and the universities, electronic publishing exploded--newspapers, e-zines, and current information sites. Of these formats, newspapers have the longest history of electronic publishing. Fifty years ago, newspapers were sent by broadcast radio to tens of thousands of home facsimile machines costing from $50 to $ 100. There have been attempts at Videotex (delivered over phone lines to home TV sets), and companies like CompuServe began offering electronic editions of national newspapers on an experimental basis in the eighties.

Online newspapers appear not to have suffered the fate of earlier electronic newspapers. In the early 1990s, only a half dozen major newspapers and about a dozen smaller papers had a significant newspaper product or an interactive/on-line paper on the Web or an Internet provider like America On Line. Even without an online product, hundreds of newspapers had web pages, thus acknowledging the importance of at least a minimal presence on this new media. By the mid 1990s, new online newspaper offerings appeared almost daily and practically every major paper now has some form of on-line product, and most of the larger papers have essentially put the entire paper on-line. Now, new online newspaper offerings appear almost daily and practically every major paper has some form of online product. Most of the larger papers have essentially put the entire paper online. There were 3,622 online newspapers midyear in 1997 and that number was projected to increase to 4,000 by the end of that year. However, the growth is stabilizing and approximately 100 newspapers have ceased online publication because of lack of profitability. On this issue, profitability, online newspapers confront the same economic constraints that other electronic publications faced: people's unwillingness to pay. However, current online efforts differ from their predecessors in that people are attracted to the product.

A recent survey found that 67% of online readers frequently read newspapers and magazines on the Internet. Not surprisingly, the original players in the online newspaper business tended to be from very large newspaper/publishing organizations that could cover the inherent cash-flow problems. The cost of entering this new format can be very high, with many newspapers and magazines laying out over $100 million per year to create and support electronic publications. It is apparent that many smaller newspapers have joined the Net bandwagon and are running their operation with just a few people—a new survey found that typical full-time staffing is one advertising employee, one technical employee and two editorial employees. The rapid growth of online newspapers is the most important challenge facing newspaper publishing.

Virtual Communities

The term community has a number of historical usages--e.g., developing a place with boundaries that identifies a neighborhood and thus marking who lives inside and who lives outside; or more ideologically, a coming together in social communion. Although the concept is culturally bound (for example, the conservative right in the U.S. tends to conflate community with family), the most common notion seems to be that communities are identified groups of interdependent people who discuss actions and share certain practices and have a concern for the common good. Each person, withdrawn into himself, behaves as though he is a stranger to the destiny of others. His children and his good friends constitute for him the whole of the human species. As for his transactions with his fellow citizens, he may be among them, but he sees them not; he touches them but does not feel them; he exists only in himself and for himself alone. And if on these terms there remains in him a sense of family, there no longer remains a sense of society.

According to Rheingold, "virtual communities are social aggregations that emerge from the Net when enough people carry on those public discussions long enough, with sufficient human feeling, to form webs of personal relationships in cyberspace." This definition of emergent, somewhat opportunistic, or community generated and run networks seems quite distant in time from many of the more current examples of the numerous virtual communities.

These recent examples suggest that there is a growing movement to commodify the architecture for virtual communities. One highly identifiable virtual community that has been hailed as indicative of "the new architecture" of virtual communities is "ParentSoup". ParentSoup is designed to facilitate parents' questions about raising children. They recruit "local mayors" who maintain the site's areas by ensuring that questions are answered and individual participants "feel at home". Their grass roots approach is modeled after Alcoholics Anonymous—the conversations have a "strong design" but no single voice dominates.

The parent companies of online newspapers have been interacting more closely with their local "constituent" neighborhoods and communities for the last decade. Often called public or civic journalism, this strategy is often critiqued as pandering or "journalism by polling." This focus on the market has led to a "local, local, local" business strategy for many newspapers that is now being adopted by others on the Net. The concept of building communities is not exactly a new idea. Local newspapers, trade publications, interest-based magazines, and local television and cable markets have been in this business for a long time.

Besides pandering, the other major concern many publishers have with public journalism is perceived conflict of interest. Newspapers are supposed to explain the community, not convene it. News reporters are supposed to explain the issues, not solve them. Newspapers are supposed to expose the wrongs, not campaign against them. The response to this position is that a newspaper can be involved in helping nurture job growth and otherwise creating a more vigorous neighborhood without having to buy in to public journalism; however, without a strong economic base the newspaper will cease to exist. Thus newspapers must build their own communities—by working to renew civic life and support local mom and pop businesses—if their papers are to survive. The notion that "growing communities" is a common business strategy for print newspapers leads us to ask, what variation on the theme might be operationalized in an online newspaper organization?

The original online paper had only about 5% content overlap with the print version of the newspaper. The Paper explicitly marketed (both internally and externally) the online newspaper as a completely separate product with articles, features and pictures not found in the newsprint version of the paper. As with other newspapers that had aligned themselves with a online service provider, The Paper reformulated its publication strategy and moved to the Web in 1996. This service/product was taken off-line for four months and reorganized as a "shovelware" product on the Web. In the process of moving to the Web, the newspaper eliminated 2/3 of the positions for the electronic paper although it is beginning to increase its staffing again.

Moderately-structured interviews were the principal data collection means. Interview questions focused on the leadership strategy, communication issues, and the internal cultural changes related to the adoption of "electronic newsroom" technology and services. The New Media group's members, executives and strategic planners, individuals from sales, advertising, and information systems, and the head of communication for the organization. All interviewees were told that their responses would be kept confidential. Interviews with more than half of the original staff of the electronic news service, including the managing editor and his boss, were supplemented by interviews with newsroom reporters, and the controller and CEO from the parent organization. The research team was also given copies of all the official internal and external announcements surrounding both the initial online news service and the move to the Web. These included letters from the publisher, press releases, press kits, news stories, the internal communication plan for employees and training materials designed to acquaint employees with the Internet.

Additional interviews continue to be conducted with members of other newspapers undergoing similar shifts to interactive newspaper publishing, in order to provide additional contextual data and update the literature review in an arena that is undergoing extremely rapid growth and change. All interview responses, field notes and documents were shared with all members of the research team. Results are organized around two dominant themes that emerged through an analysis of the data: changes in print journalism production practices and changes in business strategy models.

Changes in print journalism production practices. Unlike other types of online news providers, newspapers have been slow in recognizing that a fundamental condition of effective Web communication is interactivity. Most of the reporters interviewed were horrified at the idea that readers would send them e-mail about a story they wrote and might even expect an answer. In fact, the initial online service that was available on Prodigy did not have chat rooms or any direct links back to authors or editors (although the e-mail addresses of a few of the executives could be retrieved through some significant search efforts).

One of the members of the online staff claimed that the journalistic culture is really not suited to interactivity—that most of the reporters were interested in telling the world what was going on, and creating a compelling account of events. This is consistent with McAdams' account of helping the Washington Post's online service. Her position is that "A journalist with little on-line experience tends to think in terms of stories, news value, public service, and things that are good to read, but a person with a lot of online experience thinks more about connection, organization, movement within and among sets of information, and communication among different people."

Newspapers continue to act as if people only go online to get information, ignoring the fact that some of the most successful online sites like America Online's The Motley Fool attract people to a dynamic community that brings them back time and time again. Another change in production practices is a turn toward a broadcast, rather than print journalism model of operation. The computing editor of the San Jose Mercury News stated that the key to understanding the online newspaper organizations that are not following the architecture of The Paper and are providing users with up-to-the-minute reporting is the increasing stress related to instantaneous reporting. When the organization perceives its greatest competition to be CNN's Web site, then updating information becomes a 24-hour per day job as opposed to a newsroom's daily deadline. In such an environment there are serious questions about finding the time to ensure accuracy, much less build community.

While the Web is clearly about blending boundaries between media (adding video, audio, etc.), and making access to information as seamless as possible, the strategy of The Paper is clearly not one of opening space but of confining it. In the midst of a global network, this newspaper is busy constructing what we call "virtual geographic space." The reasons are strictly economic at one level and about image construction at another. In their move from Prodigy to the Internet, the business model changed from a pay-per-subscription service to one where advertisers pay for space, form, and placement for their ads on the screen. In this model, the longer the time someone spends "inside" this site, the greater number of ads the customer is likely to see and the larger the chance that an ad is actually clicked on as a "destination" during the reader's stay in the site.

One of the most obvious ways the online newspaper can maximize ad exposure and time spent inside the site--and thus increase their advertising rate--is through the use of contests, games and activities that can only be accessed by clicking on an advertisement icon. This practice of creating their own space is also consistent with the recent finding form the latest Interactive Services Survey. Even though there has been a great deal of hype about partnering, newspaper Web sites are do-it-yourself projects. "Fully 68% of responding newspapers say they take less than 20% of their overall Web site content from outside sources". The much less obvious approach involves getting users to their site and not letting them leave.

The New Media organization is also attempting to leverage The Paper's name and image as a key regional source of information and create a "gateway" to their virtual colony. By creating a series of pages and sites that includes everything that has to do with the metropolitan region, even information that is not traditionally in newspapers but more akin to information from a convention bureau or chamber of commerce, The Paper increases the probability that they can attract users to their site and then keep them there.

The result of this colonization is a series of what we see as protectionist behaviors as the overall business strategy moved from a developmental orientation to one of acquisition and coalition. Although we had been told initially that the New Media organization was attempting to be very innovative, fewer and fewer employees believed this to be descriptive of their organization as the study progressed. For example, according to several interviewees, Web sites that were originally going to be created in-house were eventually purchased on the recommendation of the advertising members of the cross-functional marketing strategy team. In addition, The Paper is actively working with competitors to set up "standards" that will protect them against the vagaries of technological advances.

While most papers think of local competitors and national competitors, online newspapers are now talking about web competitors—and they are usually not talking about the electronic services of other newspapers. When competitors for that "virtual geographic space" begin to produce their own content (e.g., Slate, Microsoft's online magazine), then the online newspapers' competitive edge against AOL and other providers of news—superior content—becomes threatened. As a result, this organization is acting like a "defensive prospector" —pushing hard to be out in front, and kicking and screaming all the way. Although many of the other newspapers have started down similar paths, we came across several recent reviews of online sites and strategies that announced The Paper had the best model for online newspapers. There are more daring models available: for example, the Raleigh, North Carolina, News & Observer's nando.net helps students create their own content.

In the last twenty-five to fifty years, print newspapers, "arguably the archetype" and "prototype" of all modern mass media, have been slipping from their prominent place in American lifestyles. This decline, as measured by a number of different indicators, has been dramatic. Similarly, some states that "newspaper editors and publishers have been aware for some years that their audience, if not actually slipping, is not keeping pace with the growth of the population". Others writes that "for millions of Americans, especially young ones, newspapers have never played a significant role", and that this is but one aspect of the larger problem, that "newspapers have been foundering for decades, their readers aging, their revenues declining, their circulation sinking".

Rising costs of producing and distributing a paper compound print newspapers' problems. The price of newsprint has tripled in the past twenty-five years. Distribution of newsprint papers has become increasingly complex. Adding to the problems of circulation declines and rising costs, newspaper advertisers, a large source of newspaper revenue, have been pulling their business from papers to invest in advertising strategies with more focused and/or total penetration possibilities, like direct mail or distributing to shoppers. With the increasing popularity of the World Wide Web as a consumer-oriented mass medium, one strategy for addressing print newspapers' problems has been to move the genre online. This movement proceeds at a dizzying pace. Outing notes that 100 commercial newspapers existed online, worldwide, at the beginning of 1995, a number that grew to 750 by the beginning of 1996, to 1,115 by May 1996, and to 1,587 by December, 1996.

Moving newspapers online is seen as a strategic move to both retain and expand a base audience of print newspaper readers. Rationales for this strategy, based on assumptions about the audience, are outlined below. First, moving newspapers online might recapture young readers, who have fallen away from the habit of reading hard-copy papers, and yet may be attracted to online services. Some notes that younger readers "have grown up with computers and video games"; perhaps they'll grow into the newspaper habit, online. Erlindson observes that "Online newspapers are the newspapers [sic] way of reaching at a younger audience".

Second, moving newspapers online facilitates immense archival capabilities, and these archives, along with tools for quickly and conveniently searching and retrieving from them, are assumed to be attractive to the online audience.

Also, moving newspaper production and distribution online is promised to eliminate, or at least alleviate, much of the cost associated with newsprint production and distribution notes that "Electronic publishing is a marriage between low manufacturing costs and an expanding consumer market". Moving newspapers online also removes traditional space restrictions, allowing for greater in-depth coverage of items of reader interest.

One last characteristic of online news assumed to be of value to its audience is interactivity. Many commentators note that moving newspapers online allows readers, writers, and publishers to interact more directly than ever before. Some defines this interactivity as "facilitating discussions or figuring out how to involve audiences meaningfully in gathering information," or even in "actively helping readers create their own content". Hume defines online interactivity similarly, saying that this feature can allow the audience to collaborate in newsmaking. Hume also predicts that successful online papers will be those that allow for "talk back" features, allowing the audience to voice their opinions of newspaper coverage.

Claims about the advantages of moving newspapers online are grounded in assumptions about the online audience. However, for such claims to be valid-and any related hopes for newspapers' economic viability to be realized- an understanding of the audience is necessary. Such an understanding would encompass what that audience looks for in an online paper, and what they do with what they find.

One way to develop an understanding of online audience motivations is to start with an appropriate theoretical framework. Some commentators have called for a theoretical grounding in new media studies. Specifically, Williams et al. suggest the mass media theory of uses and gratifications as holding particular promise for the study of new communication technologies like "video cassette or disk, cable television, new telephone services, home computers, videotext or teletext services". As many of the forecasts about online newspapers are based on assumptions about their audience's uses and gratifications, it does seem that uses and gratifications theory might be a suitable framework for testing these assumptions.

Further, uses and gratifications theory incorporates both the online and the newspaper characteristics of online newspapers. Print newspapers are traditionally considered to be mass media. The Internet, too, has been categorized as a mass medium.

In addition to being historically applied to mass media study, and thus applicable to considerations of both newspapers and online media, uses and gratifications is a receiver-based communication theory. In fact, almost any consideration of media from a uses and gratifications standpoint explicitly asserts as its central maxim the idea of an active, rational, goal-seeking audience. Uses and gratifications studies as "concerned with (1) the social and psychological origins of (2) needs, which generate (3) expectations of (4) the mass media or other sources, which lead to (5) differential patterns of media exposure (or engagement in other activities), resulting in (6) need gratifications and (7) other consequences, perhaps mostly unintended ones".

Related to this central assumption of an active, goal-driven audience is the assumption that the audience selects from and uses various media and non-media "functional alternatives." Functional alternatives provide audience members with alternate means of achieving the same ends.

Methodologically, uses and gratifications research assumes that audience members are self-aware enough to report on their personal motivations for using media. Most uses and gratifications studies, with their reliance on calculations and self-reporting as data-gathering techniques, accept the validity of this assumption. A reliance on empirical research design, and multivariate statistical analysis and techniques, are also central in the uses and gratifications tradition.

One final tenet of the uses and gratifications tradition is the belief that "value judgments about the cultural significance of mass communication should [or at least can] be suspended while audience orientations are explored on their own terms". Uses and gratifications research, then, sometimes suspends value judgments about cultural implications of media use in order to explore audience activity on its own terms.

Uses and gratifications research has been subject to criticism for some of its assumptions. First, the tradition has been criticized for a "tunnel vision" focused so exclusively on the audience's actual mediated communication experience that other substantial concerns have been ignored.

Palmgreen also defends the tradition against criticisms that it is "atheoretical." Though such charges may have once had merit, Palmgreen asserts that by the mid-1980s they would be "difficult to defend". For, according to Palmgreen, by 1984 uses and gratifications research is in a late phase, one of "theory development," which "is concentrated on attempts to provide explanations of the ways in which audience motives, expectations, and media behaviors are interconnected".

In particular, Palmgreen identifies six main strands of research evident in uses and gratifications studies, and proposes a theoretical model that integrates all of them. These six practice strands are: "(1) gratifications and media consumption; (2) social and psychological orientations of gratifications; (3) gratifications and media effects; (4) gratifications sought and obtained; (5) expectancy-value approaches to uses and gratifications; and (6) audience activity". Of particular interest to the pilot study reported below is the fourth research strand Palmgreen identifies: a consideration of gratifications sought and obtained.

In terms of print newspaper reading practices, six participants responded that they'd read a print newspaper the day before; nine had not. Two participants say never reading print newspapers; seven respondents reported reading print papers 1-3 days per week; three respondents reported reading print papers 4-6 days per week; and three respondents reported reading print papers every day.

Participants' mean time for reading a daily print paper was 23.71 minutes; for reading a Sunday print paper, 38.2 minutes. Seven respondents had access to print papers via a household subscription; one respondent subscribed individually; four respondents reported usually buying single issues at a newsstand or store; one respondent reported usually reading papers received for free; and two respondents did not report their primary access to a print paper.

These demographics are, in some respects, not particularly representative. The sample is, however, useful and appropriate for a pilot study. Moreover, many of the characteristics represented here are precisely those that online newspapers find attractive in a potential audience, including proportionately high incomes and low ages. The predominantly male makeup of this sample reflects the predominantly male makeup.

Modifications are planned to increase both the size and representativeness of the sample in the online newspaper study. And, though the sample size is relatively small, participants in the pilot study are representative of a range of print paper-reading practices. Thus, information from the pilot, and the follow-up online newspaper study, may illuminate motivations of both non-print newspaper readers, and those who read print newspapers with varying frequencies.

The online newspaper activity was structured as follows: First, the participant was given an orientation to the activity, and asked for their consent to participate in the study, and to be video- and audio-taped. If the participant gave consent, video and audio recording equipment was started, and the participant began the (up to) twenty-minute activity of viewing an online traditional newspaper.

Participants were given a selection of two local and two national online newspapers. If participants preferred, they could select any other World Wide Web (WWW)-based newspaper. As the participant engaged in the viewing activity, the video recorder captured every screen movement. The audio recorder captured the participant's think-aloud protocol. After twenty minutes (or when the participant decided to stop, if sooner, the participant answered an interviewer's questions about the activity.

After another brief orientation, participants viewed their personalized Crayon newspapers for up to fifteen minutes. Again, a video camera recorded screen activity and a tape recorder captured the participant's think-aloud protocol. And again, at the end of the activity (at fifteen minutes or when the participant chose to stop, if sooner), the participant answered an interviewer's questions about viewing their Crayon.

Three datasets were thus gathered:

1. Data about participants' opinions and uses of both print and online newspapers;
2. Video recordings of participants' online traditional and online personalized newspaper-viewing activities; and
3. Audio recordings of participants' think-aloud protocols as they engaged in the online newspaper activities.

The video data has been fully transcribed, and analyzed to any extent. Videotape data was transcribed and coded into several variables for tracking participants' online newspaper activities. These variables included measures of the types of screens participants viewed; subjects viewed; time spent viewing a screen; time spent waiting for a selected display; etc.

To test for hypothesized relationships, Spearman correlation coefficients were calculated for pairings of behavioral data, as follows: In testing H1, predictor variables were audience self-reported measures of print newspaper gratifications, correlated with criterion variables of audience self-reported measures of online newspaper gratifications. Drawing from uses-and-gratifications literature, eight gratification categories were elicited via survey measurements. These eight gratifications include:

1. avoidance; that is, negative gratifications or disincentives to consume news media;
2. entertainment;
3. escape;
4. excitement;
5. parasocial interaction; that is, affective gratifications related to some sense of social interaction gained from media consumption;
6. relaxation;
7. surveillance; that is, "knowing what's going on in the world";
8. and utility; that is, perceived direct usefulness in some matter such as forming opinions, making plans, or making decisions.

The items operationalizing each gratification were drawn from prior uses and gratifications studies. Table 1 lists the items used to operationalize each gratification category.

Table 1. Gratification categories and items.

Gratification: Avoidance

— Newspapers don't give enough information about the information I'm interested in.

— Newspapers include unpleasant information.

Gratification: Entertainment

— It's fun to read the newspaper.

— Reading the newspaper cheers me up.

— Reading the newspaper is enjoyable.

Gratification: Escape

— Reading the newspaper helps pass the time.

— Reading the newspaper is an escape from loneliness.

— Newspapers provide diversion from school, work, or other things.

Gratification: Excitement

— Newspapers carry personal ads.

— Newspapers contain some exciting news and features.

— Newspapers contain stimulating information.

Gratification: Para-social Interaction

— Newspaper writers give a human quality to the news.

— Writing a letter to the editor is like talking to other newspaper readers.

— Newspapers are a way to learn about other people's opinions.

Gratification: Relaxation

— Reading the newspaper is a way to unwind.

— Reading the newspaper is a way to relax.

— Reading the newspaper helps me fall asleep.

Gratification: Surveillance

— Reading the newspaper is a way to learn about people and places far away.

— The newspaper is a source of current information.

— The newspaper is a source of trustworthy information.

Gratification: Utility

— Reading a newspaper is a good use of time.

— Information in newspapers helps people decide what to buy and where to buy it.

— Information in newspapers helps people plan their evenings or weekends.

In testing H2 and H3, predictor variables of audience self-reported measures of both print and online newspaper gratifications were correlated with criterion variables measuring audience online activity. Online activity was measured in terms of time spent viewing different subjects.

Online Journalists

The burgeoning online newspaper industry is creating both

excitement and fear among journalists and their audiences. Little is known or predictable about these new media ventures, despite the constant attention they receive. With the number of online newspapers increasing every day, there is a growing demand for online journalists. According to the Editor & Publisher Web site, there are more than 1,000 online newspapers in the United States. Some say there are as many as 10,000 online journalists.

The term "online journalist" is now acceptable even though those journalists complain about the lack of respect accorded them. Some found that not only are more journalists joining online ventures, other journalists are increasing their use of the Internet. Like many new ventures, the online components of many daily newspapers were set up as separate entities. Berkman found that many Web staffs were created by newspapers who didn't think their print staff could handle cyberspace ventures.

Cox Interactive Media, which among its sites publishes online versions of the Atlanta Journal-Constitution and Austin American-Statesman, believes that the online venture has little in common with its print counterpart. Most online staffs also are significantly smaller in number than their print counterparts. The *New York Times* online-the New York Times Electronic Media Co.employs less than 25 journalists.

While many issues of trade publications and journalism reviews contain articles about online journalists, little is found in scholarly journals about these pioneers. Studying these early online journalists can provide some answers about what the online newspapers are doing and who they are depending on for the success of their online ventures. It also may provide some guidance for journalism programs eager to place graduates. Recruiters visiting schools of journalism two years ago were excited to see the occasional student-designed Web pages. Now, having a Web page is a given. Students' resumes and clips are expected to be online.

And students often report being frustrated by the lack of specific information they are given about what the recruiter is seeking in terms of journalistic and computer skills. Often, students say, the online employers say they are seeking the traditional skills of good reporting and writing, analytical skills and visual literacy. And, they add, knowledge of HTML, PhotoShop and the ability to create a multimedia story incorporating text, graphics, hypertext links, audio and even a basic understanding of how to put video online. While today's online journalists are learning on the job the next wave will be expected to have already learned the skills they will need to succeed online.

There is, however, concern that the emphasis on technology may dissuade some from pursuing these careers. Although excitement about the online newspaper industry and demand for personnel to produce these sites is high, there is little known about who is producing these online ventures.

There is no shortage or shyness of opinions about what online newspapers and online journalists should be doing. Some critics even argue that those two words-online newspapers-do not belong together and that to succeed on the Internet, a news product needs to be very different than its print counterpart. The possibilities for interactivity even may create a new type of celebrity journalist. At the very least, the Internet should facilitate more communication between journalists and their audiences.

To that end, critics say it only makes sense that journalists have to change. If that is true, it portends changes in the structure not only in newsrooms across the country, but within any journalism program that also wants to stay in business. It seems to follow, then, that to understand online newspapers, there is a need to examine the journalists who create them. Who are they? What is their background? What skills do they say are important to doing their job? How satisfied are they with their jobs? This study is a report of what journalists at 13 online newspapers say is important to doing their job, how they like what they are doing and what they see themselves doing in five years. It also provides a snapshot of who they are.

The Online Newspaper Industry v. its Print Counterpart

It seems most everyone has an idea about what and how information on the Internet should be presented. While some media professionals worry that the Internet will usurp traditional media, most agree that the Internet is not yet what it needs to be . Among the 20 million or so Web users, most have some idea of what they want to see on the Internet. So far, it's not "news" as the media traditionally define it. One critic argues that if "Way New Journalism" is to succeed, it will need to disregard most of its print counterpart's methods. "The day the *New York Times* tells us all the news that's fit to print is over. Its era of dominance has passed because the world has changed".

Yet, one of the lessons from the history of media technology is that journalism evolves and journalists adapt. Print reporters in the 1940 and 50s became early broadcasters, page compositors became paginators in the 1980s and surviving through it all were newspapers. It appears unlikely that online newspapers will soon replace any existing media. Like those early days of other media, however, the online media industry is attracting pioneers who are eager to try their skills in the new ventures.

Newspapers are in a unique position to compete in this new environment. Despite what some may view as their stodgy ways, they still command a lot of resources. "It takes a lot of money and talent to put out a quality product," admits one online publisher. Others agree that in the undisciplined world of cyberspace, such journalistic skills as writing objectively, verifying information, and creating a context for information may be even more valuable.

There are limited areas of agreement as to what online journalism needs to encompass. Taking advantage of technical capabilities, such as interactivity and multimedia, are areas of agreement. How best to do that is, of course, an area of disagreement. At the same time as there is extensive attention being paid to the new media ventures, there is growing malaise about the traditional journalism career. While Stepp attributed much of the discontent to increasingly business-driven decision-making, others say the problem is more complex. In their longitudinal study of journalists, they have documented changes in the general characteristics of daily newspaper journalists. They report that the median age for all journalists is now about 37, with those 35-44 constituting the largest age group. In addition, women now make-up about 34 percent of the workforce, and for those with less than 10 years of experience, women are nearly 38 percent of the staff.

Nearly two-thirds of the participants in their calculations have been exposed to some journalism education, with 84.3 percent possessing a college degree. Their study also shows an average salary of just over $35,000. One of their most significant findings is that job satisfaction among all journalists is declining. Only about 25 percent said they are very satisfied with their jobs, a 50 percent decline from 20 years ago.

It is interesting to note that among the factors these researchers say lead to greater job satisfaction is one that may have more success among online journalists: feedback from the audience. Journalists in the study also indicated that getting information to the public quickly is extremely important to them. That also would be an advantage for online journalists.

Although Weaver and Wilhoit did not specifically poll online journalists, they note several other points that seem to pertain to online journalists: A small, but significant, shift is apparent in the transmission role, as more journalists see that as highly important as compared to a decade ago. the biggest change, though, is the decline among those who place high value on reaching the widest audience.

Both these changes likely reflect technological developments that enhance the speed of information processing and the fragmentation of mass audiences into specialized markets. While the growing dissatisfaction with traditional paths is being documented, some argue that the growing online industry may have a favorable effect on print newspapers. If that is the case, the online journalists will have an even brighter future.

In general, online journalists reflect many of the demographics found by Weaver and Wilhoit in their studies of journalists. There are, however, differences in their level of job satisfaction and the skills online journalists say are important to doing their job. The respondents' time at their online newspapers seems to correlate with the age of the online newspaper. More than half of these online journalists have been at their jobs less than a year. The online papers ranged in age from two months to 36 months. Just over half the respondents say their newspapers have been online for only 16 months. The most common age of these ventures is, in fact, one year (20.5 percent). However, there are a number of newspapers that have been online 18 to 30 months (38.5 percent). For nearly 70 percent of the respondents, this is their first job with any online venture. However two journalists told the author that they felt they had been working in the online world since the early 1980s when Dow Jones launched its News Retrieval system. They pointed out that this system and other proprietary Dow Jones online ventures had been providing "real time" stock reports for decades.

Table 1. Length of time online for newspapers and journalists

Months	*% Newspapers Online*	*% Journalists Online*
0-6	7.7	7.0

7-12	25.6	38.5
13-17 5.2	0.0	
18-24 28.2	12.9	
25-36 18.0	15.5	
more than 36 months	0	2.6

Most of the respondents also said this was their first online job; only 12 percent said they had worked at another online site and only 2 respondents said they had worked at another online newspaper. They found that somewhat surprising given the anecdotal stories about job-hopping in the online environment. The number of online staff members at most sites is quite a contrast to their print counterparts. Considering the size of the staff at most of these newspapers, the number of people working with the online newspapers seems very small.

Perhaps the area that seems more inconsistent with what critics say the online newspapers need to be is the skills that these online journalists say are important to doing their job. While critics say online newspaper need to write concise, compelling and interactive stories to engage the audience, these online journalists rank spelling, grammar and punctuation skills higher than generating story ideas.

Editors told the author that their need for online journalists with good editing skills was one reason for their participation in an internship program which focused on editing. The online editor at *The Minneapolis Star Tribune* emphasized that sloppy editing jeopardizes the credibility of online newspapers-just as it does in the print newspaper. While these online journalists said grammar skills were very important (56.4 percent), only 25.6 percent said generating story ideas was very important. And 30.7 percent said generating story ideas was not very important to unimportant!

Yet, respondents agreed that knowing about their audiences was important (66.7 percent). Several online editors told the author that their Web sites consist mostly of material "repackaged" from print. They expect that to change to an increased emphasis on original content. They predict the online journalists' ability to generate stories will become increasingly important. Consistent with their view of the importance of grammar skills are the importance these journalists seem to attach to other areas that are usually associated with editing functions. 64 percent said headline-writing ability was important to doing their jobs and 62 percent said writing concisely was important.

The importance attached to these skills appears to reflect what journalists said during their interviews were their main jobs-rather than creating original content, these journalists are "repurposing" material from the print version, wire services and other sources.

Online journalists also reported that analytical thinking was important (72 percent), as are computer skills (62 percent). It is interesting here to note, however, that more than a quarter of the respondents (26 percent) said computer skills were not very important or unimportant. Respondents also were somewhat less inclined to think of computer design skills as important, with 46.2 percent saying such skills are somewhat important.

Table 2. Skills online journalists say are important to doing their jobs

Skill	*Important-Very*	*Neutral*	*Less-Unimportant*
Knowledge about Web	69.3	10.3	20.5
Spelling, grammar,etc.	74.3	5.1	20.6
Computer skills	61.6	12.8	25.9
News judgment	74.3	2.6	23.1
Know about audience	66.7	12.8	20.5
Computer design	30.7	46.2	23.1
Headline writing	64.1	15.4	20.5

Story ideas	46.1	23.1	30.7
Analytical thinking	71.8	12.8	15.4
Writing concisely	61.5	10.3	28.2

Among other traditional newspaper skills ranked high was the need for the ability to make news judgments. Nearly 75 percent (74.3) ranked it as important to very important. The managing editor at *The Wall Street Journal* Interactive told the author that sound news judgment is an invaluable skill, no matter the journalists' environment. It is rather interesting , however, that 23 percent said news judgment was not very important or unimportant to doing their job!

Most of the online journalists also report feeling positive about the future of online newspapers and their futures with online newspapers. When asked how they view the future for online newspapers, 69.3 said they felt very positive (30.8 percent) or positive (38.5 percent). No one reported feeling negative about the future, although 28.2 percent said they were uncertain. That optimism is reflected in what they say they will be doing in five years, with 74.3 percent saying they will be working for an online product, either an online newspaper (41 percent) or another online product (33.3 percent).

The majority of them also are satisfied with their jobs with the online newspaper Nearly 75 percent said they were either very satisfied (43.6 percent) or highly satisfied (30.8 percent) with their jobs. They also felt most people doing similar jobs were satisfied, with slightly less (66.7 percent) enthusiasm. Most of them (76.9 percent) also said they would even encourage others to do similar work. And, they believe this type of work is what news people will be doing in the future (79.5 percent).

Interestingly, however, the greatest agreement comes in response to being asked about the fear of technology. Nearly all these journalists (97.4 percent) say that fear could prevent someone from doing their type of work. The demographics say these online journalists are reflective of the general population of daily journalists, as reported in other studies. They are male (64.1 percent), have less than 10 years of newspaper experience (53.8 percent), have an undergraduate degree (94.9 percent) typically in journalism or a related field, and do not belong to any journalism organization (87.2 percent). While the largest group is the 31-39 years olds, 38.5 percent of them are under 35 years of age and 28.2 percent are 40 or older.

Also, the greatest number of them (33.3 percent) report making more than $50,000 annual salary. Although that salary is higher than the average reported in other studies, it is important to again note here that the journalists responding to these questions are employed by major daily newspapers in metropolitan areas and as such, would be expected to have higher salaries than the norm. Discussions of salaries and hiring often brought up the subject of unions.

During many of the informal discussions at these sites, editors spoke of the unions as one reason for their "independence" from the print newspaper. At the *New York Times Electronic Media* Co., the online venture is housed in a building miles from the parent company. The online venture has a great deal of autonomy in hiring and the online journalists do not have the longevity of journalism experience one might expect of an editorial employee. The online supervisors of these interns told the author that it would be "extremely unusual" for the editorial departments of their print newspapers to hire anyone seeking a first job.

Nearly half said they would like to be able to share thoughts with other online journalists about their skills, experiences and expectations. It also appeared they were eager to find out what other online journalists were thinking, especially since as one respondent put it: "We're so busy and there aren't enough of us to do all the work that we don't have time to reflect much on what it is we are doing."

Online journalism is in its infancy, although some argue it ought to be at least toddling along by now. Yet, little is known about who is working on these online newspapers. Other than anecdotes about famous journalists moving into the online realm, don't have a good picture of what these journalists view as important to doing their online jobs, how they feel about their work or even how they compare demographically to other American journalists.

Studying these journalists at this point in the development of online newspapers helps provide a better idea of the product. In understanding these journalists, a better understanding of their product emerges. Future studies might compare online content with the training, experience and skills of the site's producers. The author intends to continue to use her access to participants in the editing internship program to track online journalists.

Important concerns are the attitudes online journalists have about their role in a democratic system, what training they feel is important to succeed in the online environment and how the relationship of the online site and print newspaper will evolve. Another concern of online research concerns how responsive an online site should be to its audience. In this new media environment, data detailing audience behavior can quickly be analyzed. What will dictate content-the news judgement of online journalists or the content tallying the most "hits"?

Several online journalists who spoke with the author expressed concern that the online world would have a version of a rating system in which sports and entertainment get higher ratings news. After visits to these seven newspaper sites and three non-newspaper sites, it appears that there are different factors driving Web development. Future research also needs to correlate who is creating these sites with the "vision" of those making development decisions.

Online Coverage

It is still too soon to definitively identify the Web's effect on the American electorate in 1996. After the 1992 campaign, there was a great deal of talk about candidates' use of nontraditional ways of reaching the public, from MTV to radio and TV talk shows; in retrospect, it appears that print and TV news continued to play a more potent role in the campaign than the newcomers.

But in 1992, "online newspapers" consisted almost solely of a few pioneers offering small-scale electronic versions either as stand-alone products or through such commercial services as Prodigy or America Online; they were very much still feeling their way, and their audience was, perhaps mercifully, minuscule. Studies that have sought to assess the impact of online information on the election, have necessarily considered newspapers as separate and distinct from computer-based media forms rather than as contributors to them. Indeed, it is only very recently that researchers have begun to view the Internet as a "multifaceted mass medium" at all and to start to evolve conceptual and theoretical approaches for studying the 'Net and its audience.

However, initial reactions to the much-anticipated Year of the Web indicate that, at least in terms of the electoral process, it wasn't. True, more than 800 commercial U.S. newspapers had ventured online by the end of 1996, along with hundreds of broadcast and cable TV networks and affiliates, dozens of specialized political information sites such as PoliticsNow and Project VoteSmart, and countless candidates from the presidential level down.

Most Americans either didn't know or didn't care. A Pew Research Center found only 3 percent of its respondents went online more than once a week for campaign information; a Media Studies Center found that only 6 percent ever visited a politically oriented site.

In the meantime, newspapers did offer extensive online coverage of the '96 campaign, and they tried plenty of innovative things in the new medium. Early analysis of Web users during the primary season, for instance, indicates the people who visited political sites were news junkies with a higher-than-average level of interest in the campaign anyway. Researchers continue to tally the effect of online political information on voters in the general election, but early returns indicate it may have been minimal.

Newspapers with Web sites are still too new a phenomenon to have generated much published research into the nature of online competition, but a considerable amount of work has been done, particularly by Lacy and his colleagues, on how a diversity of media voices affects the news product. The consensus seems to be that the more media outlets, the greater the diversity of content-but only up to a point that lies within boundaries established by journalists' similar news judgments and publishers' similar financial constraints.

However, some researchers suggest the differences may be greater than previously supposed. Of particular interest here is that the surviving paper, devoted almost a third of its news hole to political stories, running nearly twice as many political stories as its competitor during the study period in the mid-1980s.

Somr pointed out, there is considerable evidence that while the average citizen has access to more diverse sources of news than ever control over that news is in the hands of fewer and fewer institutions. Information may come from more places, but it is often the same information in different packages. Of particular relevance here are two studies recently published in Journalism & Mass Communication Quarterly. First, some found that the presence of more newspapers in a county leads to closer election outcomes, especially in open-seat contests in which no incumbent is running. Newspaper journalists-who at most papers are responsible for producing Web site content- believe competition promotes editorial diversity, competitiveness for stories and increased sensationalism. But as the authors suggest, the fact that hometown dailies are no longer seen as the only "real news" source for their communities creates fertile ground for research into the nature of intermedia competition. This study of how two competing papers used the Web to cover the 1996 election hopes to offer a step in that direction.

Two complementary methods of data collection were used in this study. The primary method was a content analysis of both the print and online versions of the Denver Post and the Rocky Mountain News during three selected weeks in August, October and November 1996. The goal was to assess the scope of political coverage in each medium, so that they could be compared and contrasted. In addition, interviews were conducted, in person and by telephone, with the newsroom editors in charge of the online products at each of the two papers.

The three one-week periods during the general election campaign "season" selected for study-each a Friday through a Thursday, partly in order to incorporate complete weekend coverage and partly for news reasons-were not chosen at random.

Friday, Nov. 1 through Thursday, Nov. 7. This period surrounded Election Day, Nov. 5. It took in coverage of the final stages of the campaigns, including the last stormy debate between the candidates in Colorado's U.S. Senate race. Inclusion of the Wednesday and the Thursday papers after the election captured both election-night coverage and the day-after summaries and analyses that the two papers provided.

For each of these weeks, two sets of data were gathered. One set consisted of all U.S. election-related items in the local and national news sections of the early edition of the printed Post and News, plus political editorials, op-ed columns, cartoons and letters on their editorial and op-ed pages. These items were recorded and categorized using a coding sheet that accommodated such information as story source, length, accompanying graphics and category. In all, 774 election news items were identified and coded during the three weeks of the study: 354 from the Post and 420 from the News. In addition, 89 editorials and op-ed columns, plus 34 editorial cartoons and 65 readers' letters were identified and coded from the Post, as were another 89 editorials and columns, 46 editorial cartoons and 61 letters from the News.

The second set of data consisted of printouts of the home pages and the political content offered by the online versions of the Post and the News. The author accessed the online papers at roughly the same time during the afternoon of each day of the selected weeks. The News did not have a separate section for campaign coverage, so any relevant stories were simply printed out. The Post offered a "Colorado Campaign" section that included both daily updates and archives of previous stories; both the day's new items and the menus of archived material were printed.

In all, 116 election-related news items were identified and printed out from the two online papers: 35 from the News and 81 from the Post. Because almost all of these items also appeared in print, they were not individually coded in the same way. Rather, they were analyzed for any differences between the printed and online versions, such as changes in headlines or text. When the online version offered items that were not in the print paper-such as the full text of the presidential debates linked from a story in the online News—these were also noted.

Table 1

Total Number of Political News Items in Sample Weeks

	August	*October*	*November*	*Total*

Printed Post	49	92	213	354
Online Post	13	20	43	76[1]
Printed News	79	94	247[2]	420
Online News	11	12	12	35

1] In addition, the online Post ran four op-ed columns, written by the paper's staffers, during the three weeks; it also ran its own editorial endorsements, beginning Nov. 3. Those five items bring the total number of online items to 81.

2] The News also ran a 32-page pull-out Election Guide as part of its Sunday, Nov. 3, paper. The Post's Election Guide ran during a week not included in this study; the number above does not include stories in the News' Election Guide because their inclusion would create an inaccurate impression of the comparability of coverage by the two papers. As a point of information, the News' guide contained 91 stories, consisting primarily of candidate profiles and answers to questions about their stands on various issues; and 29 infographics, such as maps of Colorado's congressional districts, boxed descriptions of contested offices and a sample ballot.

Because of the transient nature of online content, it was not possible to perform reliability tests on this material to ascertain whether all political items had been identified when they appeared. In addition to this analysis of the print and online products, interviews with Post and News journalists involved in the Web sites were conducted on Aug. 6; Oct. 18; Oct. 23; Nov. 13; and Nov. 20. Notes and, where available, tapes of these interviews were transcribed and used to provide insights into the nature of competition, online and "offline," as well as the reasons behind decisions reflected in political coverage on the Web.

Probably what is most immediately obvious is that the sheer volume of election-related information offered in the print papers dwarfed what was available online on any given day. The goal of this study was not to detail differences between the broadsheet Post and the tabloid News, although the data do lend themselves to follow-up statistical analysis along those lines. But the raw numbers indicate that in print, the two competing papers were roughly comparable in their political coverage-with the News taking a numerical edge attributable mainly to more short items about the presidential contest and a greater emphasis on Denver-area races, in line with the paper's marketing strategy of pulling back to circulate almost exclusively within the metro area.

Online, however, the differences between the two papers were considerable, as were the differences between each paper's own print and online versions. The News, which offered 616 political news and editorial-page items in the print paper during the three selected weeks, ran just 35 election-related items online during the same period, or around 6 percent of the political content in the paper. The Post offered more online content — 81 unique political items during the three weeks but still less than 15 percent of the 542 total news and editorial-page items related to politics in the print paper.

The reason for the difference between the two online versions was apparent from visits to the two newsrooms. A three-person team worked on the online Post: a former political reporter and long-time city editor who was in charge of the online service; a recent college journalism graduate who worked as a consultant, handling updates and helping develop new content; and, as of late September, an online advertising executive. At the News, the copy desk was given the task of updating the online service at some point in an already-busy evening; the person in charge of the online product was the deputy managing editor, whose main job was to get the printed paper off the floor every night.

The News' philosophy was to use the Web to complement the print edition, so online content tended to have "shelf life"-a recreation guide, entertainment information, background on the city's pro sports teams. "Politics is clearly an area that you want to get involved in. It's very central to what newspapers do. But some limitations that we've been faced with in terms of manpower and also equipment have not made that a primary area," he said. "We're trying to do as much as possible with as little as possible."

In the meantime, the primary advantage over print that the Post offered those seeking political information online was an extensive archive of stories about the presidential, senate and congressional races in Colorado. A story might run on the Post's home page or at the top of its online "Colorado Campaign" section the same day it appeared in print, then move to the appropriate archive spot, creating a running account of developments in key contests.

Both the Post and News also offered hypertext links to additional material available online. The Post's site included a standing section called "On the Net," with links to candidates' home pages, national political news sites such as Politics Now, and sites offered by major national news organizations such as CNN and The New York Times. However, the Post did not incorporate those links within its stories; users had to return to a menu page and work their way back down. At the News, links were more sporadic-but when they were offered, they were associated with specific, related stories. For instance, the day after the second presidential debate, the News used an AP story, then ran links down the side to items ranging from the complete text of the first and second debates; Clinton and Dole home pages; a site offering audio from the debate; and another site that afforded opportunities for user participation in forums and polls.

But aside from such impossible-to-ignore news stories as the political conventions and the debates, both the online Post and News focused almost exclusively on staff-written stories. In the printed Post, election items during the selected weeks included 151 wire or syndicated news stories and 203 staff-generated items or stories written for the Post by correspondents or special contributors.

Online, the Post ran only three wire or syndicated election news stories, compared with 78 staff-written items. Similarly, the News ran 189 wire and syndicate election news items in its print editions during the study period and 231 staff-generated items. Online, it offered 29 staff stories and six from the wires. In addition, the op-ed pages of both print papers contained a mix of local and syndicated items. Aside from an occasional op-ed column by a Post staffer, neither paper ran editorial or op-ed pieces online.

Neither the Post nor the News editors said they had heard any complaints from reporters about the online products. Interest varied among individuals, they said, but newsroom reaction was generally favorable. Because the online editors at both the Post and the News got the stories after they already had been through the copy or city desk, they seldom took advantage of the lack of space limitations online by running stories longer than the printed versions. In the rare instances in which stories were longer online than in print, it was either because two or more stories had been merged into one or because additional background information had been inserted into the online version.

The headlines were different in print and online because of varying counts. What's more, differently worded prompts led to the same story from different spots in the online Post's structure. Because of the desire to allow users to access items from a variety of archival locations, a single story might have several pointers within the Web site.

Another key difference between the online Post and News was their use of graphics. The online Post contained no photos; its main menus, including the home page and the Colorado Campaign page, offered standing logo-like graphics, but lower-level menus and stories were text only. If, as visual communication research suggests, images play a strong role in helping people evaluate and form opinions about political candidates, those cues were entirely lacking in the online Post.

The News always runs a large photo or graphic on its front page, along with a series of references to inside stories, and that format was carried over to its online product. A large color news photo appeared online daily- though the online photo was not always the same as the print photo. Of the 21 days included in this study, the online photo contained political content 11 times, compared with six times in print.

It has become axiomatic among Internet aficionados that this, at last, is a medium to fulfill the dream and the promise of a society resonating with a true multitude of voices. Editors at both the News and the Post expressed regret that the technology available to them did not allow creation of discussion forums and other interactive structures that would enable the sort of citizen involvement in the electoral process that is a key aspect of the civic journalism movement. They simply did not have the resources to begin to build a structure that allows "a collection of views to be archived, reread, explored and connected in new ways that offer new models of problem solving that expand the narrative boundaries of traditional journalism".

The Internet has recently blossomed in Latin America. Non-government organizations have stepped up efforts to develop a Latin American backbone, to extend telephone connections and spread Net literacy. Scholars regularly communicate with colleagues worldwide. For-profit companies offer connections; publications devoted to cyber issues have cropped up.

Cybercafes populated by the young and Neterrati proliferate in major cities. Some of the recent earth-shaking political events in the region, such as the Zapatista uprising in Chiapas, Mexico and the takeover of the Japanese embassy by a guerrilla organization in Peru, have had a decisive presence in cyberspace. News agencies offered gavel-to-gavel coverage, chat groups extensively discussed latest alternatives and political implications, and supporters have created websites to announce the demands of the insurrects.

The Zapatista webpage, which includes communiques, news, interviews, photos, archives and instructions for potential supporters, has received a lot of attention. Most discussions have focused on the opening of a new front for the old information and propaganda battles between governments and insurrectionary forces. Some have argued that Internet communications made possible the building of global support and international pressure that successfully prevented the Mexican government from escalating operations against the Zapatistas.

As the Internet has grown, the worldwide stampede to online journalism has not spared Latin America. Throughout the region, all major newspapers and a substantial number of smaller publications have launched their digital editions. Having started operations between 1995 and 1996, an approximate total of 120 dailies currently offers online editions. Additionally, commercial television and radio stations, weeklies and monthlies, and a myriad of grassroots media organizations provide news services.

In the most populated and economically developed countries of the region, the number of news organizations in the Internet has swelled. Fifty dailies based in Brazil and Mexico, over forty percent of the total in the region, produce online editions. This remarkable growth should not be surprising as, in a different scale, it mirrors the formidable global rush to "inkless journalism." According to current estimates, over 1,700 newspapers now offer online services, fifty-seven percent of which are based in the United States.

In this context, it is argued, the motivations and expectations for starting digital editions are different among Latin American news organizations. The second section reviews the content of online news and suggests that digital dailies reinforce the hierarchical structure of newspaper markets in Latin American countries. Economically stronger news firms can devote more resources than medium and smaller companies to online editions and, consequently, have more possibilities to explore novel ways to produce news taking advantage of several media technologies. Digital dailies recreate and maintain a sense of national belonging among Latin American diasporic populations, the largest readership of online editions.

The Latin American case is intriguing for the explosion of digital news is taking place in countries where Internet access is significantly more limited than in the developed world. Despite renewed enthusiasm in policy and academic quarters about the capacity of new communication technologies to reverse global information inequalities, the actual expansion of the digital revolution in Latin America still falls short from the forecasts. It remains to be seen whether the latest round of innovations will effectively allow the region to leapfrog several stages in technological development and "catch-up" with the developed world. Much of the unbound optimism about "virtual" technologies contrasts with the "real" situation.

No doubt, domains and hosts have geometrically increased in the last year. Latest figures report that over 130.000 hosts are currently functioning in Latin America. The Internet, however, has not evolved evenly throughout the region. Fifty percent of all hosts are located in Brazil where the Net has grown exponentially in the last three years. Also, the rates of hosts per 1,000 inhabitants widely varies, ranging from 1.3 in Chile to 0.004 in Cuba and the

Dominican Republic. Other countries with the highest density are Costa Rica with 1.1, Uruguay with 0.6, Argentina with 0.455, Brazil with 0.28, and Colombia with 0.269. These numbers pale in comparison to, Finland or the United States.

These figures indicate that the size of the Internet population continues to be rather small compared to North America, Western Europe, Australia or Japan which, according to latest calculations, concentrate fifteen percent of the world population but comprise ninety-eight percent of available hosts. Although most researchers agree that it is extremely difficult to gauge exactly the number of users, available calculations estimate the number of Net users in Latin America is over one million.

The main reason for the limited expansion of Internet services is the region's weak information infrastructure. Telephone systems have been notoriously underdeveloped. Touted as a sure solution to expand penetration, the privatization of formerly state-owned telephone companies in many countries has yet to change dramatically the historical low percentage of functioning lines. The regional average is 7 lines per 100 inhabitants.

Central America has an average of 6.5 but density rates range from 1.9 to 14.2. Similarly, the low number of personal computers limits Internet access. The regional average is between 2 and 3 percent, much lower than the PC population in the United States where approximately one-third of households own computers or than in other developed countries where rates range between 7.75 (Italy) to 19 (Canada). The rate of penetration for all Central American countries, below 1 PC per 1000 inhabitants. Moreover, telephone connections continue to be plagued by problems that make Internet connections difficult and, at times, almost impossible. Despite recent renovations, most systems are outdated and unable to effectively service rising demand and traffic.

Aside from an inadequate infrastructure, low computer literacy and high costs for commercial Internet subscriptions make unlikely a substantial expansion in the number of users. Persistent socio-economic and educational inequalities definitely put a cap on the possibility of throngs becoming Internet users anytime soon.

For a vast majority of citizens, cyberspace remains an unknown and remote space. It is hard to predict a dramatic turnaround when large numbers of people are still living below the line of poverty and public schools and libraries (which potentially could provide free access to those who lack PCs, telephone connections and/or means), have been chronically underfunded and are in dire economic straits.

If the numbers of Internet connections and users continue to be modest, albeit growing, why have major and smaller news organizations jumped onto the Net in Latin America? Neither great expectations about millions of readers joining the Net in the short- or medium-term nor the promise of bountiful economic goals have driven the decision to set up online editions.

Limited technological, economic and educational resources in Latin American societies dampen whatever optimism might exist about vast numbers of Internet users. These limitations, in turn, make it difficult to have high hopes about turning digital editions into money-making ventures. If skepticism about their potential profitability still persists in the developed world, the region's unique problems shed further doubts on the commercial prospects of such enterprises in the developing world.

The business calculations of major news organizations in developed countries hardly translate to Latin American dailies. The decision to offer digital editions did not respond to a "defensive" strategy, as it has been argued about newspapers in the developed world. That strategy refers to the decision to produce digital news to protect news companies from a foreseeable hemorrhage of print advertising, mainly classified ads, dailies' economic bloodline.

There are no visible threats in the Net that might damage or even shave the advertising prowess of the newspaper industry. Fewer numbers of Internet connections and users coupled with sponsors' mild interest on online editions as advertising conduits determine that the economics of the media industry, more than in the developed world, still favor print newspapers.

Nor was the decision an "anticipatory maneuver" to stave off potential competitors for advertising monies. More than two years after the first newspaper began with digital news, online editions still have little advertising and only a few offer classified ads, the bloodline of their sister paper editions. Only a handful of newspapers display ads, mainly banners and logos of software and hardware companies. The dailies which feature advertising as well as up-to-date and more expensive designs are divisions of media powerhouses. Without expectations of drawing massive readerships or high hopes of a bright commercial future, newspapers decided to offer digital news for other reasons.

For horizontally integrated companies, the move onto the Net was expected, a relatively low investment to secure a slot in a new media environment and thus, reinforce multimedia aspirations. No one seems to know for sure what the future of news will look like. Initial forecasts about the demise of print news and the glory days ahead for digital news seem to have lately turned into more mixed conclusions and prognoses that predict coexistence with "at least in my lifetime" caveats. As uncertainty persists, staking out a lane in the information superhighway while learning the ropes of the new media is a preventive measure.

Latin American dailies approach digital news as a way to tiptoe into a new technology. Some already had Bulletin Board Systems in function, others started cybereditions as the Internet experienced a substantial growth in 1995 and

1996. Curiosity and a me-too mentality played a part. No one wanted to feel left out of a novel form to deliver news, regardless of its commercial potential.

Having incorporated computers in newsrooms and satellite for national distribution of complete or partial editions during the last decade, cybernews seemed a logical follow-up step, especially for those dailies that prize themselves at being at the forefront of technological innovation. Aside from other goals, getting presence on the Net is a matter of image, a badge of honor to display as a sign of forward-looking, cutting-edge companies.

For the editor of Argentina's La Nacion, the online experience is a way "to strengthen our image as a modern newspaper". There is certain pride associated with having online news. Print editions often boast the popularity of the paper's Webpage and announce the different services offered. Weeks after its first online issue, a full page in El Tiempo, the leading Colombian daily, reproduced a dozen of e-mail messages mostly signed by academics praising the daily for its cybernews.

Not all newspapers devoted similar resources to launch and maintain cybereditions. Although actual numbers on investments are tightly kept, editors recognize that they are considerably lower than what US dailies have allocated. Resources vary according to the overall size of the economic and financial structure of the press firm. To put it differently, online editions reflect disparities in the economic muscle of news companies as well as the different expectations of news organizations in branching out to a new technology.

Generally, small and provincial newspapers kept start-up costs and operational resources minimal while larger dailies allocated more monies. As analyzed below, these dissimilar investments are expressed in the characteristics and innovations featured in online dailies.

Although they are still undergoing an initial phase of experimentation while the contours and uniqueness of the new medium remain undefined, not all online editions are identical. For most newspapers, the Internet is mainly an instrument to branch out without having to introduce significant transformations in the character of news or existing reporting practices. It provides a new outlet for delivering information produced for the print version rather than an opportunity to refashion the production of news or to reconsider the role of journalists.

Large information and entertainment groups invested substantial monetary and human resources. The digital edition of Folha de Sao Paulo, the leading Brazilian daily, is part of Universo Online owned by the Folha group. In October 1996 it merged its online service with Brasil Online, owned by group Abril whose flagship is Veja. It is the largest digital service in Latin America feeding 220 channels from 24 stations. Its staff of 80 people is divided in four areas: Content, Technology, Business, and Development.

If wide differences in resources allocated to cybernewsrooms indicate that dailies hold different expectations and interests about online news, then, it is not surprising that the content and services they provide greatly vary. Seemingly, the priority was "to be on the Net" rather than to maximize the possibilities that the new medium offers or to experiment with new roles dailies might have in an electronic environment.

The content of online editions in contemporary Latin America suggest a rich diversity of experiences that do not fit conclusions applicable across the board. Little is produced anew and online staffs mostly edit content and readjust recycled news to the requirements and nature of the technology. The sheer size of the audience of traditional media and, possibly, a journalistic culture that still privileges old media account for why cyberjournalism is conceived as an ancillary medium. As the editor for digital edition of La Prensa from Panama puts it, "the online edition is still secondary and subordinated to the regular edition".

No major transformations have happened yet in terms of news content. Most online services basically shovelware information from print editions while granting only minimal concessions to the new medium. Many dailies do not even include photographs, much less hypertext or sound. Content is edited with shorter texts and more space between paragraphs to avoid long scrolls, and headlines are rewritten to fit better space constraints. The information, however, often duplicates print news. A brief review of different aspects of online content indicates that only a few newspapers have flexibilized news production and explored the technological possibilities of the Net.

1) *Immediacy:* Rarely do dailies take advantage of immediacy, widely touted as one of the key advantages of cyberjournalism. Most online editions close soon after the print edition does and no changes are incorporated throughout the day. Breaking news is rarely reported first on the Net. Only during big news events, elections or accidents, is digital news published first. In general, however, it is unlikely that cybernewsrooms would scoop their sister print publications when the latter still command larger audiences and advertising. This reflects that digital dailies are still not a priority for most news firms. The exceptions are the digital editions of the major newspapers. With stacatto, wire-like writing, Folha Online or Clarin's sports section regularly update information without waiting for the morning edition to hit the presses.

2) *In-depth news:* Another added-value of cybernews is in-depth reports. Without limits imposed by advertising, an endless newshole allows the inclusion of information often shortened or discarded from print editions. Ideally, news articles are unlimited as

background information or links to related subjects can be provided and reporters can include thorough research in their stories. Readers have the possibility to construct news using different bits and pieces of information not necessarily produced by the digital paper they have originally picked to read. The virtual reality, however, is distant from the potential. The use of hypertexts linking articles to other sites, databases and archives on related subjects is extremely rare. Online papers rarely churn out original stories. The basic reason is the lack of staff fully devoted to producing stories exclusively for the online edition. Only a handful of digital dailies, and on a few topics, expand coverage and bring information unavailable to print readers. Again, the editions of major newspapers are the exception as they have more reporters working in digital newsrooms.

3) *New news:* To its most enthusiastic advocates, digital dailies introduce the possibility of customized information, offering localized news and features of specific interest to their readers. The majority of Latin America has yet to deliver these new newspapers. Only a few online editions tailor news content to the demographic profile of Net users or take advantage of digital technologies to produce news differently. The Mexican newspaper El Norte, one of the best expressions of investigative journalism in Latin America, has expanded its hard-hitting style onto the Net. Its online version published information obtained from computer diskettes that belonged to an attorney linked to drug lords who was shot to death. Clarin Digital displays several online-only sections: a file on soccer information, an encyclopedia of Argentine rock music, a children's section, photographic views of the city of Buenos Aires and the main newsroom, news radio broadcasts, surveys conducted among online readers, and chat rooms mediated by invited guests.

It is one of the few digital newspapers in Latin America that actually produces hybrid news mixing video and audio.

4) *Interactivity:* Lastly, electronic papers make possible two-way, person-to-person communication between newsroom and readers. All editors for Latin American online papers acknowledge that they receive a substantial number of e-mail messages. Readers frequently send suggestions and comments, some of which have been incorporated. They are skeptical, however, about a more interactive relationship between "content providers" and readers that could dramatically change the traditional division of roles as it exists in old media. Only few reporters have e-mail accounts yet, those who do, are usually overloaded with work responsibilities and have no time to answer to readers' queries. Understaffed newsrooms do not have time to develop one-to-one conversations with the public. Nor does there seem to be a strong pressure from readers to redraw the boundaries between them and reporters: one editor observes, "readers still behave like readers of the print edition".

Online content shows two main characteristics of Latin American digital dailies. Generally, they are not different papers compared to print editions. Also, there is a widening gap between big and medium—and small-sized newspapers. Backed by stronger reporting structures and corporate might, the largest dailies have been exploring different possibilities and aiming to offer news that do not simply recycle print editions. This breach reproduces the different presence of the firms in the print and the information markets at large, suggesting that the coming of new technologies allows big media companies further horizontal expansion.

Reimagined Communities

Despite differences in terms of number of staff and content offered, Latin American digital dailies may actually have a similar function as "home away from home," that is, being able to regenerate and solidify national sentiments. They serve as sources for emigres to come in regular contact with their homelands. Although there are no precise figures about where readers are geographically located, online staffs acknowledge that expatriates are a substantial percentage of the total number of virtual readers. This comes as no surprise given the difficulties examined above in regard to the situation of Internet connections in Latin America and relative ease of becoming connected in the developed world. Reportedly, most online readers live in the US and Canada.

The weighty presence of expatriates has encouraged newspapers to adapt content and functions of online editions. Los Tiempos has opened a file for Bolivians living abroad to register. El Comercio Online from Ecuador features short contextual and historical pieces to frame current news as the majority of its readers are Ecuadorians living abroad and may be unfamiliar with events and names.

The decisions to launch digital editions were informed by a mix of curiosity and business expectations rather than by the intention to provide a cultural network for expatriates. But like colonial newspapers that, were "appendages of the market" yet articulated an early sense of national belonging among "fellow-readers" in Spanish America, digital dailies may similarly bring together dispersed readers and recreate a national consciousness. It would be wrong to see this as a case of new technologies creating national communities ex-nihilo.

Online news offer ways to strengthen already existing national identities among diasporic populations. From a ritualistic view of communication, digital dailies help to maintain social and cultural bonds. As they provide spaces for expatriates to meet and interact, whether on chat rooms or as a result of regular exposure to same news events, digital editions continue to draw and flesh out national boundaries. The Internet, often seen as the space of no-space, reinforces identities, experiences and memories attached to a distinctive geographical space and allows a continual reinvention of imagined national communities.

The coming of digital dailies has generated a number of questions regarding the changing roles of "content providers" and the future of print media. Frequently, observers rhapsodize about new media technologies and the possibilities they offer to change radically news reporting. What they forget is what a number of critics have indicated: how social and political powers shape the introduction of technological innovations, how changes gradually take place, how responses tend to be essentially conservative to the threats that new technologies pose on existing structures and dynamics.

Having these considerations in mind, it would be shortsighted to understand new technological developments without a clear diagnosis of journalism's problems and strengths. It is necessary to ask whether online news would offer ways to remedy the shortcomings of journalism.

Journalism's job is unlikely to change significantly: it's likely to remain as the institution dedicated to pick, process and interpret news. Even when online editions feature original documents and testimonies in full length and/or hypertext linking to alternative/ complementary/related sources, newsrooms would still cull, filter, package and produce news.

One of the main challenges is whether online editions can offer possibilities to rethink the character of news and effectively contribute to disseminate information not available elsewhere. Would routines that essentially produce standardized news be different in online newsrooms? Would "news" be dramatically different? Are digital dailies likely to focus less on authoritative sources and enlarge the diversity of voices? Would investigative journalism, a healthy and growing development in Latin America during the last years, find room on digital editions to tackle diverse controversial subjects and widen the reporting lens? Or is muckraking antithetical to online news given the latter's emphasis on immediacy? Would digital news be the same news but delivered through taking advantage of technological convergence and unlimited newshole?

A good number of Latin American newspapers produces online editions yet their different approaches to cybernews makes it difficult to reach general conclusions. Current digital newspapers do not affect journalistic work similarly, introducing new dynamics or changing the characteristics of news, in all newsrooms. For reporters who produce original material for online editions, the growth of digital news opens up new questions about the character of news, the construction of stories, the possibility of collaborative work with people with different expertise, and the relation between journalists and readers.

This is exceptional, however, as most digital newsrooms edit, rather than originally produce, material published in the print version. Unlike online editions of US newspapers, the demands on the staff of online services are not greatly different than for print reporters as methods of news gathering and news production continue practically unchanged.

More importantly, generalizations a la "online news would not change journalism" might overlook different technological, social, and economic contexts as well as the fact that newspapers, as the Latin America cases reveals, have developed different online news editions. These factors greatly shape the functions, services, and potential of cybernews.

4

Electronic Newsgathering

The influence of geography on newsgathering, just as the influence of geography on any culture, is inescapable. Accidents or imperatives of geography shape every civilization, every institution. In any society, geography influences the foods that are eaten, the clothes that are worn, the gods that are worshipped, the language that is spoken, the physical and mental traits that are valued and rewarded. That is no less true of journalism than it is for any other culture. For centuries, the geographic relationship between the journalist and the sources of news has been simple: The journalist was required to go where the information was located. Because that is what reporters did, that is what reporters became: People who went searching for news, and who defined news by what they found in their travels.

As one contemplates the traditional practice of journalism, even at its most elementary levels, geography comes immediately into play. One of the five basics of news writing, taught to every beginning journalist, is to state where the news occurred, and to preferably include that information in the lead paragraph of the story. This emphasis on place in writing is closely connected to the concept of proximity, which is classified as one of the key determinants of how important a story is deemed to be. Simply put, the closer the story to the reader, the bigger the news. Thus, as anyone who has ever been spent time in a newsroom knows, a bus wreck in Russia is less "newsworthy" than a bus wreck next door.

Geography also plays a more subtle role in the determination of what constitutes news. Specifically, is "news" simply the reflection of activities and events that occur in the natural world? This would seem to be Allen's view and the view of many journalists. If so, journalists would be required to transport themselves to where these events are happening because there would be nothing else on which to report. Sports reporters, largely follow this model. They don't cover games on the radio or television, they go see for themselves. Political reporters assigned to conventions and legislatures go directly to the locus of newsmaking activities because they have little choice, although Congressional reporters increasingly use C-Span to assist in their coverage of daily floor activities.

Most contemporary analysts would argue that this view of news as being the simple reporting of naturally occurring events is much too simplistic. Instead, they see news as being a construct in which reporters assemble "news" from a variety of parts-the statements of sources, the observations of the reporter, tempered by the reporter's judgments and values, the professional work of the journalist in producing stories, the business needs and aims of the publication or broadcast outlet. Journalists, particularly investigative journalists, long have seen the reporting function as being more than a transcription of events, arguing instead for the power to probe beneath the surface of events in order to provide context and meaning. News, in this construction, is something that, like ore, has to be prospected for, mined, recovered, and processed. To describe themselves, journalists speak, in admiring tones, of the "digging reporter," who unearths gems of information. To be a reporter, then in this construction, was to be a troubadour, a seeker, a wanderer through life. This person was required to pause frequently to determine whether he (or, increasingly, she) was in the presence of news.

This system of newsgathering, in which the journalist was expected to seek out sources, to interact frequently with a diverse set of individuals, helped determine the type of person who was attracted to the pursuit of reporting. It placed a high importance on the personality of the journalist. One thirty-year-old textbook says, "The reporter should develop as many sources of news as possible.

This requires that he be gregarious - that he develop a friendliness with the stenographers and clerks in the public offices as well as with the officers themselves". Other traits useful to reporters, according to the text, are curiosity, a critical sense and resourcefulness. In other words, the emphasis was placed largely on the instinctive or intuitive abilities or powers of the journalist; conversely, less attention was paid to the analytical or intellectual skills that might be employed.

In deference to the physical reality that a person cannot be in more than one place at the same time, beats were born to facilitate coverage of a particular location. Working through these beats was part of the way that beginning journalists were trained in the craft and by which they were inculcated in the traditions and culture of the news business. Generations of young reporters have cut their journalistic teeth making the daily rounds of the police station, the courthouse, city hall, the federal building, and the other places where sources or potential sources reside, waiting to impart wisdom to the enterprising journalist.

Geography helped define the standing and prestige of journalists inside news organizations. Once the technology of the telegraph helped give rise to the system of bureaus in state capitals, Washington, and major cities of the world, being assigned to one of those distant locations became a career goal. "Washington is the goal of every political junkie, the pinnacle for journalists fascinated by the human hodgepodge we call government.

The chance to cover Washington should be and often is the reward for distinguished reporting at city hall or the statehouse," former Washington journalist Don Campbell writes in "Inside the Beltway," his study of reporting in the capital. The foreign correspondent, played so dashingly by Hollywood leading men, became a romantic ideal-proving that reporters would go to the ends of the earth to hunt for news and, not incidentally, be rewarded for their quest for truth with the embrace of beautiful women.

For those still tied to the home office, travel became an accepted part, even a sought-after part, of a reporter's life. Journalists with the freedom and portfolio to travel were envied; beats that came with room to roam were considered plums. In more penurious newsrooms, fights over denied travel requests often provoked or fueled reporters' enmity toward management. Long before the advent of the Internet, publishers, hoping among other things, to hold down travel costs, embraced the telephone, and the facsimile machine as ways to connect journalists and sources. Journalists rightly claim that on-site reporting is an invaluable newsgathering technique. Indeed, for many types of stories, it is indispensable. However, the reality also is that this need, or desire, to go where the "news" is made has shaped journalists' perceptions and definitions of news.

Specifically, news became what sources said it was, giving them considerable practical control over what was reported or not reported. Thus, the role of the journalist became passive, not active. Reporters in this mold are mirrors, not analysts, of information they receive. This role, as it happened, melded neatly with the emerging economic pressures that made objectivity the orthodoxy—the unchallenged way to practice journalism.

Geography shaped the definition of news in other ways, as well. Stories about government agencies and politics became paramount because it was to government buildings that journalists went to find news. Bush, defines beats as "those public places in which news events are recorded (e.g., a police station) or in which public affairs news develops (e.g., the city hall)". Using this traditional definition of the locus of news, much potential news was ignored, at least partly because the places where it occurred were invisible to the typical journalist. When editors have recognized that this approach leaves large parts of life uncovered their attempts to bring about change have run into resistance from the entrenched culture.

The energy-related economic troubles of the late 1970s and early 1980s were poorly reported in part because newsrooms had few reporters or editors with knowledge about, or interest in, business and economics. Later, it was not until the savings and loan crisis became a political crisis that it made front pages and evening news broadcasts in most cities. In this sense, journalists, limited by their culture, gave proof to the adage, "Out of sight, out of mind."

It would be wrong, of course, to argue that the accidents of geography are the lone forces shaping the culture of news and newsgathering. The public needs to have the trained eyes and ears of journalists present at important, interesting or entertaining events if it is to make sense of the welter of details that surround them. Making the rounds of government buildings is an important way of gathering news, and it has many benefits.

Official sources have a right, and a need, to get their messages across to the public. Government actions shape the lives of every citizen. Unwatched bureaucracies become weak and corrupt. Unnoticed officials become unresponsive. Additionally, physical presence sometimes can provide ways to verify information collected by other means of reporting. Some stories just cannot be written without personal observation.

Pre-digital journalists could gain an advantage over their competitors by traveling to the site of information. For example, to see paper copies of campaign finance reports, one must go to a state capital or to the Federal Election Commission headquarters in Washington. Before the data were computerized, those were the only places those records were accessible.

The result, of course, is that few reporters outside the cities where the records were housed ever used them, and that millions of readers/viewers were denied the benefits of the so-called "public disclosure" of campaign records.

The Internet's "virtual geography," in which the sense of "place" loses much of its meaning, causes much of the "travel advantage" to disappear. In many instances reporters will not be able to "go" where the information is because there is no place to go, or if they do make the trip, they will find it provided them with no benefit. Take again, the campaign finance files provided by American University.

The files are physically stored on a computer in Washington, DC. But they could, literally, be anywhere in the world with scarcely any disadvantage to any potential user. Where, then, do you "go" to obtain this data? The short answer is nowhere, or anywhere. It simply does not matter, because you have virtually equal access from anyplace.

Coming to Washington would provide a journalist no special advantage when it comes to getting this data. Indeed, it would take far more time and be far more costly to travel to the data "location," than to use a computer and Internet connection at home. Even if the decision to travel to the data were made, the journalist would have access to nothing she could not have acquired in the place she left.

There are other drawbacks to having to travel to get data and information. If ten reporters show up at the North Carolina Secretary of State's office at the same time to look at the same candidate's campaign contributions file, nine will have nothing to do during the time it is being accessed by one. And to the extent that the traveling journalist loses connections to her office-based resources, she is actually less efficient as an information gatherer.

Because as a virtual journalist, one can be many places at once, defying the old physical laws of time and space. A reporter seeking, background information on a corporation can cover much more ground, much more quickly by using the resources of the Internet. In a matter of minutes on the Internet, a journalist could retrieve Securities and Exchange Commission documents about the company, find the names of key company executives, discover whether federal agencies such as the Environmental Protection Agency or the Occupational Safety and Health Administration had filed actions against the company in question. Leaving the office to try to get any one piece of that information would greatly restrict the reporter's ability to find other information. In fact, as more real-time data become available through satellite imagery, journalists will be able to literally watch the whole world from the vantage of their computer monitor. Again, the value of traveling is diminished, the importance of geographical location less relevant.

For those stories that do require journalists to travel to observe an event or to do research for a story, as many still will, the online world also offers powerful new ways to work. E-mail can help journalists stay in contact with their home offices, without regard to time zones. E-mail also can help reporters keep in touch with sources they aren't seeing because they are out of town.

Background information remains readily accessible because the wired journalist is no longer constrained by the weight of the files he is willing to carry on an airplane. Archives can be accessed easily, which means fewer late-night telephone calls to sleepy librarians. Online editions can solve the familiar problem of not being able to see how a story was edited and played when journalists are traveling in an area where their paper does not circulate.

And, the deeper one goes in the hierarchy, the more reliable the information becomes. From this simple sketch it is clear that journalists traditionally have relied most heavily on the least reliable type of sources, humans. Unfortunately, too many journalists stop at the top, believing their reporting is complete when they have talked to someone on "both sides" of an issue. What computer-assisted journalism does, greatly boosted by the increasing availability of information on the Internet, is permit fuller access to the data, statistics and facts that are the raw materials of news.

Conversely, it should make journalists less reliant on the faulty memories, the wrongheaded notions, and the outright lies of our human sources. Just to give one example of how this approach improves journalism, again from the world of campaign finance reporting: The commonly held belief is that it is the cost of television advertising that is driving up the price of political campaigns. But, when the data were computerized and analyzed by Dwight Morris, then with the Los Angeles Times, it was revealed that advertising, of any type, accounts for less than a third of total spending on Congressional races. In many ways, this kind of work is the logical outgrowth of Meyer's 25-year-old notion of precision journalism. Meyer's central view is that "we journalists would be wrong less often if we adapted to our own use some of the tools of the social scientists".

By extension, Meyer was suggesting that journalists should rely more on their own research, theories, and analysis and less on their traditional sources. The journalist becomes a more important player in the development of "news," and the "source" a less important player in this construction.

Fortunately, the tools of the computer age facilitate that switch in approach. Let me cite an example from my own career. In the late 1980s, while at Gannett News Service, directed a computerized study of the nation's savings and loan industry. As part of the analysis, we recomputed the S&L financial results using Generally Accepted Accounting Principles at a time when the industry was using a flawed system of regulatory accounting that masked its true difficulties. While we had extensive discussions with experts about how to conduct this study, in the end it was our work - we were the sources. What we started with was simply statistical raw material — computer tapes containing the financial results of every savings and loan in the nation. When finished there were no sources who could give us quotes to verify our work, because no one else had done this analysis. We found, in Meyer's terms, "a more solid base of fact from which to leap". The stories we wrote and the charts we published in *USA Today* and elsewhere painted a vivid portrait of an industry on the brink of collapse. We were able to identify specific institutions that were at the greatest risk of failure.

Although many industry sources challenged the conclusions, they were not able to argue with the data or the analytical methods used. This approach unnerves many editors and reporters. One editor asked if we planned to call every S&L in the nation to verify each number we intended to publish. The answer was no, we were going to rely on the data reported to the federal government and analysis of those data.

News, in this construction, remains something to be dug out. But the tools of the news miner are changed. There is less reliance on interviews and more use of mathematics. Analyzing huge datasets, which can add breadth and depth to stories, is technically simple, though it requires new training. There can be more attention paid to the outcomes of policy decisions and less to the personalities of those who make the decisions. Journalists using computer techniques can find new ways to categorize information, methods that should permit them to do a better job of identifying the factors that determine why, some school systems do a better job educating children than others.

The day has not yet come when this kind of analytical journalism is the rule in newsrooms. In much of this work there is little romance or glory. Journalists fret over losing the human touch; many passionately resist learning and applying statistical skills; they correctly point out that much data and information is not accessible electronically, and that much of it is also subject to human errors.

Some, frankly, do not see the value of spending the time and effort necessary to conduct these analyses when a journalist could more easily "call up a couple of people" to get their views. This means, of course, that not everyone who has previously been attracted to journalism as a career will find it to their liking in the future. We will need new sets of skills, and, in large measure, that will require people with different aptitudes to perform them.

However, there are signs that the culture of the news profession is changing. One manifestation of this is that in recent years, several Pulitzer Prizes and other significant journalism awards have gone to computer-assisted reporting projects, bestowing prestige on the reporters and highlighting the value of these skills to top-level practitioners.

Publishers have invested heavily in computer resources and computer training; increasingly they are asking for computer skills when they hire entry-level reporters and editors. Perhaps most intriguingly, there also seem to be some indications that the public appreciates this way of doing journalism.

Sources of News

The news and current affairs media may themselves be influenced by how, where and from whom they source information to create their products. Furthermore, the relative influence of the media may be mitigated by public beliefs about the credibility of media organisations and media professionals. The proliferation of media outlets for news and current affairs has created difficulties in measuring audience preferences and obtaining useful hierarchies. Likewise, the evolution of variants for the news and current affairs genre and the attraction of these variants for audiences adds complexity to estimating audience hierarchies for news and current affairs content. The problems exist for industry researchers, academics and policy makers alike. Problems with estimating the audience for BBC News 24 in Britain is a case in point. In 1998, the Independent reported audience numbers for the pay TV service at as low as 1,000. Comparatively, the BBC reported 760,000 on the basis of its own research. The remarkable discrepancy is one caused by definitions and measurement and "common currency."

For example, if simply switching onto a channel or reporting having seen a news and current affairs program in "the last week" counts, then data suggest higher audience preferences for a news and current affairs source. Conversely, if a minimum time is required (or indeed time is measured using a continuous scale such as seconds of exposure), then preference data might appear small. An interesting shift in audience preferences affecting the measurement of news and current affairs exposure and observation of hierarchical preferences is clear, as well. For example, younger audiences are being drawn to new forms of current affairs programming such as comical news and current affairs. Television programs offer a humorous and sarcastic approach to reviewing contemporary news and current affairs reports in other media.

Another factor seemingly affecting news and current affairs audience preferences is localism. To the extent that a more recent local focus by these news and current affairs providers attracts audiences, survey research should pick up an associated audience shift to these providers. The "local factor" might be more obvious, however, in newspaper circulation figures. Radio, too, is losing news and current affairs audiences. Fusion Strategy reported that the audience for commercial stations during the breakfast program timeslot in the capital cities dropped from 2 million in 1990 to 1.8 million in 1999. Nevertheless, commercial and public airwaves are supplying diverse programs for diverse audience needs and, given the numbers of radio services and stations across markets, these data will not be reviewed here.

Regardless of the nature of preferred news and current affairs content, however, the medium of choice for it is free to air television in the developed world. Canadians, for example, are heavily dependent on evening TV news and current affairs with 80 per cent watching evening news broadcasts. There, 76 per cent of audiences report reading a daily newspaper as well. Only 26 per cent report reading weekly newsmagazines and 20 per cent report using the Internet. A useful approach for measuring exposure to news and current affairs in a telephone survey may be one similar to that used regularly by the Gallup Organisation in Princeton in the U.S. for different sources and media. They ask audiences to report "how often do you get your news from [source]?" with options, "every day," "several times a week," "occasionally" and "never".

Use of Internet and TV

The diffusion of newer media for information and communication including the Internet and pay TV has meant unprecedented access to news and current affairs content. Indeed, satellite delivery systems in the television industry has produced increased ease with which to deliver national and international news agendas. However evidence of prime-time national news agendas-as an assumed function of newer newsgathering technologies-had eluded earlier researchers like Goot. Concerns about the functional results of technology growth have not been limited to the role of newer media in shifting the news agenda from local to national, indeed international, foci. For example, news information runs the potential of being inaccurate or inappropriately focused as a function of being second-hand and many claims of second-hand sourcing of news and current affairs in newer media have been made: "With a fax machine, a telephone, and computer line into Nexis, reporters can attempt to cover any kind of story without leaving their chairs. Major problem - second hand info, no first hand sense of what s/he is writing about". These anxieties aside, Australia is connecting to new sources of news and current affairs with little apparent fear that the content is either locally irrelevant or from indirect sources.

Although news and current affairs sites were not identified by the research as a top priority, the possibility exists that news and current affairs consumption is expanding into the workplace (or sidelining other media used at work) as more news and current affairs consumers go on-line. Indeed, this so-called "cyberbludging" suggests that Internet use is as likely to take place at work as it is at home - no data are available to determine what proportion of Internet use is dedicated to news and current affairs in Australia, however and Internet use dedicated to news and current affairs at work is therefore also not available. Measures of Internet news and current affairs use are varied. Johnson and Kay used four sets of measures in a Web-based survey to determine "source reliance and use" of on-line news and current affairs media: "average number of hours per week on the Web, the average hours per week on political sites, the number of times the Internet has been accessed, and the degree of reliance on the Web".

Pay TV news and current affairs

After a long and tortuous introduction in Australia, pay TV is beginning to attract a sizeable audience. However, pay TV in Australia is far from reaching critical mass in its spread throughout the country. "Australia's 47 pay TV stations had only 5.5 per cent of the average viewing audience between them during evening prime time between June 27 and July 24, according to ACNielsen data as analysed by AIS Media.

In Autralia, over 1 million homes now subscribe to pay TV, of which 150,000 were added throughout 1999. In those homes, audiences are splitting their time about equally with free to air TV channels and the Australian news and current affairs channel, Sky News attracts 400,000 viewers each week. Thus, we might infer that pay TV is but a small part of the audience's overall diet of news and current affairs. Perhaps pay TV serves a special part of that diet. According to an article in Time, cable TV tends to be preferred by news and current affairs audiences during times of international crises, but is not preferred for daily news and current affairs owing to its inherently national and international character.

Audiences and Industry

Debate surrounding the role and function of on-line news and current affairs has emerged in recent industry, academic and popular discourse. Goldsborough has argued that the personalisation of news and current affairs through on-line sources may threaten the social cohesion function of traditional news and current affairs media, which in the past century facilitated shared information. Instead, personalised news and current affairs may lead to "intolerance, bigotry and xenophobia" and to stories being biased and one-sided. The leading concern, however, is that expressed by industry watchers: That on-line news and current affairs sources are siphoning audiences away from traditional media.

The fluctuation of newspaper circulations and television ratings have, in recent years, given rise to questions about whether the attraction of Internet news and current affairs sources is siphoning audiences away from traditional news and current affairs media. Recent media reports, however, suggest that free to air television news and current affairs programs may be harder hit by on-line news and current affairs sources and services. Internet is growing in its popularity for news and current affairs and that once people begin to use the Net, they use television less overall.

The Internet is identified as the great threat to newspapers. But it may not be. It may turn out to be an adjunct; another form of publishing that meshes with, rather than obliterates, other existing forms. Although, evidence of commercial pressures resulting from a gradual shift to on-line media has been reported particularly in the use of classified advertising in newspapers shifting to on-line classifieds. Moreover, "net focus" media audiences identified by typology research are Internet enthusiasts and use the Internet before turning to traditional news media.

Newspaper reading time was displaced by on-line media use but that other media activities were unaffected and that displacement occurred mainly among males and younger audiences. Nevertheless, research suggests that in cases where traditional news and current affairs media perform inadequately to meet the needs of their audiences, migration of audiences to on-line sources appears to occur. Malaysiakini.com is a case in point. As Malaysians lost confidence in their government and government publications such as New Straits Times there has been considerable migration towards use of on-line sources. Malaysiakini.com claims 116,000 readers a day, more than some established dailies. Moreover, Harakahdaily.com, the Islamic opposition party newspaper moved on-line after their paper was removed from street circulation, and the paper's circulation has increased five-fold getting 140,000 page views per day.

The argument that journalists and other news producers are out of touch with the community they serve is well established. Indeed, interviews with journalists revealed that they are more out of touch with the community than politicians and that they have become "too dependent upon politicians and their press secretaries for their daily bread between elections and too dependent upon the major political parties for news during election campaigns,". A high degree of contact between journalists employed by rival news organisations, which potentially generates an unobservable element of inter-media agenda-setting. A research has confirmed that PR people inside and outside government are primary newsgatherers of political news for TV news organisations. These "information subsidies," as he calls them, offset the high cost of news production. The problem for journalism and journalists is an over-reliance upon PR people. This dependency on sources of influence less interested in the public good than in the good of the commercial or interest enterprise, he contends, may eventually produce regard for social issues as those matters which cannot be solved as if to encourage a public and collective throwing up of the hands.

The Gallup Organization based in Princeton in the US regularly polls the public on perceptions and uses of news and current affairs and the media more generally. In one such poll taken annually, audiences are asked how much confidence they have in 15 different institutions such as the church or organised religion, the military, the courts, banks, schools, newspapers television news and so on. The question offers four possible responses including "a great deal," " quite a lot," "some" or "very little;" "none" and "no opinion" may be voluntary responses but are not read to participants. Newspapers usually rank eighth or ninth on the list and television news ranks tenth or eleventh. These findings offer this: regardless of sources of influence, relative to other institutions in society, the news and current affairs media are well down the list suggesting a credibility problem in general and perhaps, a perceived susceptibility to influence more specifically.

News and Current Affairs

Little attention has been paid to how sources of news and current affairs present issues and themselves to the media and on the effects of these presentations on media reporting. Studies about the relationship between source and news outcomes have mainly focused on selected elites, not on interest groups. Although agenda setting focuses on issue salience and attribute salience, an extension of the latter would be the delayed correlation between news coverage about elements of the issue or object and public attitudes. A further extension would be the relationship between source information and media coverage. Journalism scholarship has acknowledged sources exercise at least some influence on reporting. Especially those of elite media, may help determine the media agenda. Moreover, along with the possibility of high source impact on the media agenda, there is a theoretical basis for successful manipulation by sources of the qualities, or second level, of media messages. These manipulations may involve availability and openness to media, the simplicity of the source's message, and the consistency with which it is delivered. Finally, the appeal to traditional "news values," or what editors consider important, may aid image.

The dominant theoretical paradigm explaining why audiences seek and attend to particular media and content within media is uses and gratifications. This perspective suggests that audiences are active, goal-driven media users. Some uses and gratifications research has examined news and current affairs selection and preference and much of it provides guidance for the conceptualisation and measurement of the factors leading to particular news and current affairs preferences. The main reasons audiences might offer for preferring their particular news and current affairs sources seem to be:

— The ability of the source to meet information and surveillance needs

— Familiarity with the source
— The palatability including humorous way in which the content is presented
— The source having information personally relevant to them
— Because of the personal qualities of the journalist or presenter
— The usefulness of the source in a [local] crisis.

Questions addressed demographics, media gratifications, and media use. Media use questions asked participants to indicate the number of days per week they used different news and current affairs media and how many TV news and current affairs programs they viewed in a week. Gratifications sought questions (to which they agreed or disagreed on a five-point scale) included a list of reasons why participants used different news and current affairs sources. The authors found that students' media use and surveillance needs increased with time at university (and therefore, presumably, with education).

Moreover, demographic differences and gratifications sought were predictors of media use. Increased surveillance needs were found to result in increased use of all news media; entertainment needs were found to result in TV news and pay TV news and current affairs viewing. Current events knowledge was related to use of print media and pay TV news and current affairs only. The reasons audiences seek media and their content may, of course, differ from the results they get by selecting those media and their content. For example, that the gratifications audiences report seeking may not be the same as the gratifications they obtain. Among the reasons are audience perceptions of content and media characteristics in advance of medium or content choice. Extending uses and gratifications to a particular news and current affairs program, strong positive correlations between the gratifications sought and the gratifications obtained amongst 306 heads of households.

A recent research suggests that the news and current affairs audience loyal to particular programs tend to have clear reasons for seeking out and using them. The research further suggests that dependency upon particular sources of news and current affairs may develop over time when gratifications sought are obtained by using the particular source. In an applied sense, news and current affairs audiences may prefer their most used news and current affairs services for any combination of five factors including:

(1) the sources presented in them are easily understood and liked by the audience,

(2) inclusion of content in them that is obviously relevant to the audience,

(3) reporters or presenters use reporting styles that are rhetorical,

(4) stories demonstrate commonality between the source and the audience, and

(5) the presenter or journalist takes a stance that makes the news organisation appear more a part of the community and less an objective observer.

For example, if broadcasters want to attract the youth audiences for their news and current affairs products, while young people are not concerned with 'wider' political issues, they tend to take notice of issues impinging directly upon them such as beach pollution or the interest rate on a personal loan" and according to focus group data from a study of young news and current affairs audiences in the world. Another reason audiences tend to prefer particular news and current affairs products is the personality resident in the journalist, reporter, presenter or columnist central to that news product. The context of use is another factor affecting audience preferences for news and current affairs sources. In particular, crises provoke audience attention to broadcast sources, particularly those that are local when the crisis itself is localised. Pay TV sources such as CNN were used to a lesser extent and Internet weather sites were another nominal source of information.

Nevertheless, the Gallup Organization found that audiences have more confidence in TV news than print and that local television news broadcasts are amongst the most preferred sources of news and current affairs. The Gallup poll shows that the public's opinion of media accuracy in 1998 is virtually the same as it was in 1988. More recent Gallup poll results showed that the American public trusts word of mouth less than CNN and that public television news, local television news, and prime-time TV newsmagazines. TV news anchors are considered to be the most trusted source of news-ostensibly because the public can hear and see them for themselves. Interestingly, local TV news and prime-time TV newsmagazines were said to be more trusted than the nightly network newscasts. Print magazines scored the lowest of all media on trust, ranking with radio and TV talk shows and infotainment shows at the bottom of the list. They do trust news media presented to them by people they think they know and trust more than anonymous journalists they can't see and relate to.

Credibility Problem

Free to air television news and current affairs has oft been derided as less credible than newspapers. However, comparisons of public trust in news from TV and newspapers show that the criticisms of television stem from its infancy in the 1950s. According to American Demographics, in 1959 newspapers were the most popular and most trusted source of news. However, in nearly every year since, TV has grown in popularity and relative trust. By 1997, 69 per cent of Americans said television was their primary source of news and "53 per cent of Americans said they would believe the tube over other media, 23 per cent chose newspapers". It would seem that journalists, reporters, presenters and commentators often are blamed for inaccurate reporting and that this, in turn, fosters negative public perception about the news and current affairs media more generally. According to Sourfield, "although the hard bitten reporter of yesteryear has passed into myth, public imagination of the journalist as rogue lives on in the definition of the "modern journalist". It is unclear, however whether the lingering rogue mystique helps or hinders the media and, indeed, journalist's credibility.

The low public perception of journalists is related to journalistic practices. An example of these is the case highlighted by Media Watch which it accused Richard Carlton of plagiarism in his report on the Srebenica massacre. Apparently the story, scenes, shots, and interviews were the same as Antelope Films' A Cry From the Grave. Although 60 Minutes admits making a 15 minute version of the original 1 hour 45 minute documentary, it denies plagiarism claiming that it was given permission from someone involved with the film. However, 60 Minutes failed to inform viewers of what it had done and gave no acknowledgement in the story or closing credits to the documentary it used. Repeated use of visual material also makes the case. Another possible cause of declining credibility is the increasing dependency on public relations sources. Public relations firms routinely attempt to use news and current affairs media as a means to publicise their products.

There are three factors that have contributed to the credibility problems of the news and current affairs media: technological innovation, public relations, and journalism routines in contemporary political communication. Yet another factor affecting credibility of news and current affairs is violence. A variety of studies lends additional evidence to the problem of media credibility. Much of this evidence specifies particular factors about the audience in relation to special kinds of news and current affairs content. Channel specialisation—the degree to which the set of programs a source transmits is homogenous—was predicted to affect participants' judgments about how representative the program content was of a particular specialty, and was also predicted to affect participants' evaluations.

Channel differentiation—whether program material was presented on one channel or on different channels—was predicted to affect perceived similarity of the content". News stories seen on specialist channels such as CNN, Headline News (HNN), Satellite News Channel (SNC) or Regional News Network (RNN) rated higher on typical news attributes than stories seen on generalist broadcast network news and current affairs channels such as ABC, CBS, NBC or Fox. Participants who watched news on the specialist channels evaluated the news more positively than participants who watched the generalist channels. Participants who watched the stories on one channel rated the news stories as more similar to each other than participants who watched the stories on four channels. The most important predictor of approval for investigative reporting was general attitude toward the function and role of media in society. News and current affairs shape the beliefs of a population and construct the agenda of popular discourse. This is evident both in the fundamentally powerful work on public opinion and agenda-setting.

Agenda-setting is a well known and robust theory over the decades since its re-introduction in the 1970s. The agenda-setting process is an ongoing competition among issue proponents to gain the attention of media professionals, the public, and policy elites. Agenda-setting offers an explanation of why information about certain issues, and not other issues, is available to the public in a democracy; how public opinion is shaped; and why certain issues are addressed through policy actions while other issues are not. The main components of the process are the media agenda, the public agenda and the policy agenda; all three interrelate, however an assumption of the model is that without the media, none of the agendas could be advanced fully. On the twentieth anniversary of agenda-setting research, McCombs and Shaw concluded that recent studies suggest more than a limited effect on cognition. Under certain conditions, the media of mass communication tell us how to think about issues and, therefore, what to think.

Public opinion "remains fundamentally a communication concept" because of the "close connection of public opinion with the processes of discussion, debate, and collective decision making" revealed across two centuries of literature on the idea and "that public debate occurs mainly by virtue of interactions between elite political actors and their attentive spectators, facilitated in several important ways by the press".

Communicating Politics, examined how the professional beliefs and practices of broadcasters and their relations to political actors and organisations shape the flow of political communication. The interaction between journalists and political institutions are complex, multi-layered and the product of two criteria: pragmatic judgments of newsworthiness and audience appeal and a "sacerdotal orientation" toward the institutions of government. Public opinion as a function of exposure to news and current affairs has also explored the influence of assumptions audiences make about how news and current affairs affects the opinions of others. Surely, any consideration of public perceptions of the influence of news and current affairs must take into account how the public thinks about the role of the media on its peers-that is, others of the public.

It is commonly assumed that the media are important in shaping attitudes. "The entire study of mass communication is based on the premise that the media have significant effects, yet there is little agreement on the nature and extent of these assumed effects". The recent Australian case and controversy over broadcaster John Laws interviewing a juror illustrates concern over the potential of journalists, presenters, reporters and columnists to affect public opinion. Presumably, under the Jury Act, soliciting information from a juror is a crime because information obtained by doing so may, in part, be relayed to the public causing undue pressure on the trial system. Under the law, therefore, the news and current affairs media are viewed as having considerable influence.

Articles were coded according to specified criteria, which were concerned with the article's dependent and independent variables, method used, statistical analysis used, and effects for each variable. The study found that media effects research shows that age is related to processing ability, understanding, and attending to media, the media are a significant source of learning, and that the media can influence attitudes, and, in turn, behaviour. An approach to assessing the influence of the media on public attitudes is simply to correlate the attitudes expressed by survey participants with their use of the media. During the 1980s, people were more likely to give the media the benefit of the doubt, claims the author, and alternative sources of news and current affairs like pay TV and the Internet may be driving audiences to choose information sources based on relative credibility.

The Australian Broadcasting Authority's most recent community survey explored views on the news and current affairs and on movies broadcast on free to air television with a focus on offensive content. Concerns about news were expressed most by people in the 35-39 year age group. Categories of concern were: graphic images, bias and intrusion, scheduling of stories. News and current affairs programs tend to show unnecessary graphic images of accidents and tragedies. Focus groups found discussion about people being shot, piles of dead bodies, close-ups of dead bodies, mass graves, and so on. While the need to know was acknowledged by participants, the need for explicit images was not supported. A widespread view that reports are designed to entertain and compete. Respondents expressed concerns about repetitive graphic images, biased stories, intrusiveness and irrelevant stories. News and current affairs programs put unnecessary emphasis on personal characteristics such as ethnic background, sexuality, disability, etc."

While journalists might attempt to remove personal feelings and opinions from their stories, the sources that they use and are dependent upon may determine the extent to which journalists can present a balanced view. Despite public concern about the nature of news and current affairs presentations, recent experimental research seems to suggest that many, but not all applications of bias, inaccuracy, intrusiveness and sensationalism may attract some audiences. For example, Newhagen conducted an experiment, which involved exposing participants to TV news images that induce anger, fear, and disgust to test memory and approach-avoidance. Images that induced anger were found to be the most memorable on a latency-to-response measure, followed by those that induce fear, then images that induce disgust. The 42 university students participating in the study were first exposed to 10 minutes of news footage and asked to move a paddle either toward the TV screen depending on whether the image induced them to want to look closer or move back from the scenes. Participants were then asked to complete a questionnaire concerning their media use and attitudes toward political issues. A second videotape, 50 per cent of which contained the images seen in the first, was then shown and participants were asked to indicate which ones they had previously seen.

On the approach-avoidance measure, participants were found to approach images that induced anger the most, followed by fear, while they avoided images that induced disgust. Images that induced anger were found to be the most memorable on a latency-to-response measure, followed by those that induce fear, then images that induce disgust. TV news producers want the audience to remember certain information, this information is best preceded by images that induce anger. An experiment conducted by Mundorf, Drew, Zillmann, and Weaver attempted to establish whether exposure to emotionally disturbing news coverage affects recall of subsequent news coverage. Two groups of respondents were exposed to 10 minutes of TV news coverage. The experimental group was exposed to an emotionally disturbing news item followed by a series of innocuous news items. The control group was exposed to only the innocuous news items. A surprise information-acquisition test followed. The study found that for a 3-minute period following exposure to the disturbing news item, participants showed a significantly poorer information-acquisition score compared to the control group. No appreciable difference in information acquisition was observed thereafter.

Lang, Bolls, Potter, and Kawahara examined the effects of production pacing and arousing content on the information processing of television messages. Their hypothesis predicts that pacing will increase the resources allocated to encoding the message through the elicitation of multiple orienting responses. In addition to affecting the moment to moment allocation of resources, arousing content and production pacing are also likely to impact the ongoing level of attention being paid by the viewer to the stimulus. The model predicts that as pacing increases, the allocation of resources to encoding will increase and that arousal increases the resources allocated to storage.

A positive version with positive audience reactions for the pro side of the issue and negative reactions for the con side of the issue, a negative version opposite to the positive version, and a neutral version. Participants were assigned to one of the 3 versions. All participants were given a pretest questionnaire. After the viewing, another questionnaire was administered with questions surrounding attitudes toward the issue, attitudes toward the speaker, attitudes toward the arguments and attitudes toward the audience. Analysis showed that the differences between conditions were subtle and that a large number of subjects did not identify the side espoused by the audience based on the reaction shots as intended. However, it does appear that in some cases, audience reactions may influence viewers' perceptions of particular arguments made, especially those which are highly controversial.

A limited number of studies have been conducted concerning regional coverage of news and current affairs and public concern over local versus national and international news and current affairs foci. The role of local news and current affairs is an important one and audiences in past research have provided evidence explaining the delicate balance that must be played by news and current affairs organisations. For example, local TV news and current affairs engenders considerably high levels of trust among its viewers.

There are two areas that are highly problematic for policy-makers: regional equity and program quality. Even in some major markets, local news and current affairs suffers from a lack of options. Forde examined the effects of monopoly on information levels and diversity. She compared the newshole of the Courier-Mail from the period when it had competition to the post Daily Sun period. In the period after which the Daily Sun ceased publication and a monopoly was created for the Courier-Mail, a significant decline in both information levels and diversity in the major news section of the newspaper emerged. Given the growth of international news and current affairs in recent years, Putnis' study of news footage also raises concerns about local perspectives. Most studies of mass media and community conflict are on large pluralistic communities and small homogenous communities and they argued that "by tracing the evolution of one 'fragmented' community's experience during a ten-year period, it is possible to discern how coverage of an environmental dispute was framed in terms of the powers involved. Media reports help define a conflict and frame it for their activists.

The media, through selection of sources and placement of their statements in stories, can legitimise one perspective while withholding legitimacy from another. The concept of frames explains the legitimising of one perspective and the delegitimising of another. The frame of a message is intended to organise audience perceptions about that issue. Media frames are used to select, emphasise and present information about what exists. Local economics influence local news coverage, particularly stories of controversial issues such as the environment. In many cases, the media content is determined partly by those who finance it: publishers, advertisers, and business elites. There is even evidence of publishers assuming an active role in directing newsroom activity on issues that conceivably might affect the newspaper's revenue.

5

Peer to Peer Network

The Internet is a shared resource, a cooperative network built out of millions of hosts all over the world. Today there are more applications than ever that want to use the network, consume bandwidth, and send packets far and wide. Since 1994, the general public has been racing to join the community of computers on the Internet, placing strain on the most basic of resources: network bandwidth. And the increasing reliance on the Internet for critical applications has brought with it new security requirements, resulting in firewalls that strongly partition the Net into pieces. Through rain and snow and congested Network Access Providers (NAPs), the email goes through, and the system has scaled vastly beyond its original design.

In the year 2000, though, something has changed—or, perhaps, reverted. The network model that survived the enormous growth of the years has been turned on its head. What was down has become up; what was passive is now active. Through the music-sharing application called Napster, and the larger movement dubbed "peer-to-peer," the millions of users connecting to the Internet have started using their ever more powerful home computers for more than just browsing the Web and trading email. Instead, machines in the home and on the desktop are connecting to each other directly, forming groups and collaborating to become user-created search engines, virtual supercomputers, and filesystems.

Not everyone thinks this is such a great idea. Some objections cite legal or moral concerns. Other problems are technical. Many network providers, having set up their systems with the idea that users would spend most of their time downloading data from central servers, have economic objections to peer-to-peer models. Some have begun to cut off access to peer-to-peer services on the basis that they violate user agreements and consume too much bandwidth.

The original Internet was fundamentally designed as a peer-to-peer system. Over time it has become increasingly client/server, with millions of consumer clients communicating with a relatively privileged set of servers. The current crop of peer-to-peer applications is using the Internet much as it was originally designed: as a medium for communication for machines that share resources with each other as equals. Because this network model is more revolutionary for its scale and its particular implementations than for its concept, a good number of past Internet applications can provide lessons to architects of new peer-to-peer applications. In some cases, designers of current applications can learn from distributed Internet systems like Usenet and the Domain Name System (DNS); in others, the changes that the Internet has undergone during its commercialization may need to be reversed or modified to accommodate new peer-to-peer applications. In either case, the lessons these systems provide are instructive, as application designers, avoid causing the death of the Internet.

History of Peer-to-Peer

The Internet as originally conceived in the late 1960s was a peer-to-peer system. The goal of the original ARPANET was to share computing resources around the U.S. The challenge for this effort was to integrate different kinds of existing networks as well as future technologies with one common network architecture that would allow every host to be an equal player. The first few hosts on the ARPANET—UCLA, SRI, UCSB, and the University of Utah—were already independent computing sites with equal status.

The ARPANET connected them together not in a master/slave or client/server relationship, but rather as equal computing peers. The early Internet was also much more open and free than today's network. Firewalls were unknown until the late 1980s. Generally, any two machines on the Internet could send packets to each other. The Net was the playground of cooperative researchers who generally did not need protection from each other. The protocols and systems were obscure and specialized enough that security break-ins were rare and generally harmless.

The early "killer apps" of the Internet, FTP and Telnet, were themselves client/server applications. A Telnet client logged into a compute server, and an FTP client sent and received files from a file server. But while a single application was client/server, the usage patterns as a whole were symmetric. Every host on the Net could FTP or Telnet to any other host, and in the early days of minicomputers and mainframes, the servers usually acted as clients as well. This fundamental symmetry is what made the Internet so radical. In turn, it enabled a variety of more complex systems such as Usenet and DNS that used peer-to-peer communication patterns in an interesting fashion. In subsequent years, the Internet has become more and more restricted to client/server-type applications. But as peer-to-peer applications become common again, the Internet must revert to its initial design. Let's look at two long-established fixtures of computer networking that include important peer-to-peer components: Usenet and DNS.

Usenet

Usenet news implements a decentralized model of control that in some ways is the grandfather of today's new peer-to-peer applications such as Gnutella and Freenet.

Fundamentally, Usenet is a system that, using no central control, copies files between computers. Since Usenet has been around since 1979, it offers a number of lessons and is worth considering for contemporary file-sharing applications. The Usenet system was originally based on a facility called the Unix-to-Unix-Copy Protocol, (UUCP). UUCP was a mechanism by which one Unix machine would automatically dial another, exchange files with it, and disconnect. This mechanism allowed Unix sites to exchange email, files, system patches, or other messages.

The Usenet used UUCP to exchange messages within a set of topics, so that students at the University of North Carolina and Duke University could each "post" messages to a topic, read messages from others on the same topic, and trade messages between the two schools. The Usenet grew from these original two hosts to hundreds of thousands of sites. As the network grew, so did the number and structure of the topics in which a message could be posted. Usenet today uses a TCP/IP-based protocol known as the Network News Transport Protocol (NNTP), which allows two machines on the Usenet network to discover new newsgroups efficiently and exchange new messages in each group.

The basic model of Usenet provides a great deal of local control and relatively simple administration. A Usenet site joins the rest of the world by setting up a news exchange connection with at least one other news server on the Usenet network. Today, exchange is typically provided by a company's ISP. The administrator tells the company's news server to get in touch with the ISP's news server and exchange messages on a regular schedule. Company employees contact the company's local news server, and transact with it to read and post news messages. When a user in the company posts a new message in a newsgroup, the next time the company news server contacts the ISP's server it will notify the ISP's server that it has a new article and then transmit that article. At the same time, the ISP's server sends its new articles to the company's server.

Today, the volume of Usenet traffic is enormous, and not every server will want to carry the full complement of newsgroups or messages. The company administrator can control the size of the news installation by specifying which newsgroups the server will carry. In addition, the administrator can specify an expiration time by group or hierarchy, so that articles in a newsgroup will be retained for that time period but no longer. These controls allow each organization to voluntarily join the network on its own terms.

Many organizations decide not to carry newsgroups that transmit sexually oriented or illegal material. This is a distinct difference from, say, Freenet, which does not let a user know what material he or she has received. Usenet has evolved some of the best examples of decentralized control structures on the Net. There is no central authority that controls the news system. The addition of new newsgroups to the main topic hierarchy is controlled by a rigorous democratic process, using the Usenet group news admin to propose and discuss the creation of new groups. After a new group is proposed and discussed for a set period of time, anyone with an email address may submit an email vote for or against the proposal. If a newsgroup vote passes, a new group message is sent and propagated through the Usenet network.

The open, decentralized nature of Usenet can be harmful as well as beneficial. Usenet has been enormously successful as a system in the sense that it has survived since 1979 and continues to be home to thriving communities of experts. It has swelled far beyond its modest beginnings. But in many ways the trusting, decentralized nature of the protocol has reduced its utility and made it an extremely noisy communication channel. Particularly, Usenet fell victim to spam early in the rise of the commercial Internet.

Still, Usenet's systems for decentralized control, its methods of avoiding a network flood, and other characteristics make it an excellent object lesson for designers of peer-to-peer systems.

Domain Name System (DNS)

The Domain Name System (DNS) is an example of a system that blends peer-to-peer networking with a hierarchical model of information ownership. The remarkable thing about DNS is how well it has scaled, from the few thousand hosts it was originally designed to support in 1983 to the hundreds of millions of hosts currently on the Internet. The lessons from DNS are directly applicable to contemporary peer-to-peer data sharing applications. DNS was established as a solution to a file-sharing problem.

The namespace of DNS names is naturally hierarchical. For example, O'Reilly & Associates, Inc. owns the namespace oreilly.com: they are the sole authority for all names in their domain, such as www.oreilly.com. This built-in hierarchy yields a simple, natural way to delegate responsibility for serving part of the DNS database. Each domain has an authority, the name server of record for hosts in that domain. When a host on the Internet wants to know the address of a given name, it queries its nearest name server to ask for the address. If that server does not know the name, it delegates the query to the authority for that namespace. That query, in turn, may be delegated to a higher authority, all the way up to the root name servers for the Internet as a whole. As the answer propagates back down to the requestor, the result is cached along the way to the name servers so the next fetch can be more efficient. Name servers operate both as clients and as servers.

DNS as a whole works amazingly well, having scaled to 10,000 times its original size. There are several key design elements in DNS that are replicated in many distributed systems today. One element is that hosts can operate both as clients and as servers, propagating requests when need be. These hosts help make the network scale well by caching replies. The second element is a natural method of propagating data requests across the network. Any DNS server can query any other, but in normal operation there is a standard path up the chain of authority. The load is naturally distributed across the DNS network, so that any individual name server needs to serve only the needs of its clients and the namespace it individually manages. So from its earliest stages, the Internet was built out of peer-to-peer communication patterns. One advantage of this history is that experience to draw from in how to design new peer-to-peer systems. The problems faced today by new peer-to-peer applications systems such as file sharing are quite similar to the problems that Usenet and DNS addressed 10 or 15 years ago.

Network Model of the Internet Explosion

The explosion of the Internet in 1994 radically changed the shape of the Internet, turning it from a quiet geek utopia into a bustling mass medium. Millions of new people flocked to the Net. This wave represented a new kind of people--ordinary folks who were interested in the Internet as a way to send email, view web pages, and buy things, not computer scientists interested in the details of complex computer networks. The change of the Internet to a mass cultural phenomenon has had a far-reaching impact on the network architecture, an impact that directly affects our ability to create peer-to-peer applications in today's Internet. These changes are seen in the way use the network, the breakdown of cooperation on the Net, the increasing deployment of firewalls on the Net, and the growth of asymmetric network links such as ADSL and cable modems.

The network model of user applications—not just their consumption of bandwidth, but also their methods of addressing and communicating with other machines—changed significantly with the rise of the commercial Internet and the advent of millions of home users in the 1990s. Modem connection protocols such as SLIP and PPP became more common, typical applications targeted slow-speed analog modems, and corporations began to manage their networks with firewalls and Network Address Translation (NAT). Many of these changes were built around the usage patterns common at the time, most of which involved downloading data, not publishing or uploading information. The web browser, and many of the other applications that sprung up during the early commercialization of the Internet, were based around a simple client/server protocol: the client initiates a connection to a well-known server, downloads some data, and disconnects. When the user is finished with the data retrieved, the process is repeated. The model is simple and straightforward. It works for everything from browsing the Web to watching streaming video, and developers cram shopping carts, stock transactions, interactive games, and a host of other things into it. The machine running a web client doesn't need to have a permanent or well-known address. It doesn't need a continuous connection to the Internet. It doesn't need to accommodate multiple users. It just needs to know how to ask a question and listen for a response.

Not all of the applications used at home fit this model. Email, for instance, requires much more two-way communication between an email client and server. In these cases, though, the client is often talking to a server on the local network. Chat systems that achieved widespread usage, such as AOL's Instant Messenger, have similar "local" properties, and Usenet systems do as well. As a result, the typical ISP configuration instructions give detailed instructions for email, news, and sometimes chat. These were the exceptions that were worth some manual configuration on the user's part. The "download" model is simpler and works without much configuration; the "two-way" model is used less frequently but perhaps to greater effect.

While early visions of the Web always called it a great equalizer of communications--a system that allowed every user to publish their viewpoints rather than simply consume media—the commercial explosion on the Internet quickly fit the majority of traffic into the downstream paradigm already used by television and newspapers. Architects of the systems that enabled the commercial expansion of the Net often took this model into account, assuming that it was here to stay. Peer-to-peer applications may require these systems to change.

The early Internet was designed on principles of cooperation and good engineering. Everyone working on Internet design had the same goal: build a reliable, efficient, powerful network. As the Internet entered its current commercial phase, the incentive structures changed, resulting in a series of stresses that have highlighted the Internet's susceptibility to the tragedy of the commons. This phenomenon has shown itself in many ways, particularly the rise of spam on the Internet and the challenges of building efficient network protocols that correctly manage the common resource.

Spam, or unsolicited commercial messages, is now an everyday occurrence on the Internet. Back in the pre-commercial network, however, unsolicited advertisements were met with surprise and outrage. The end of innocence occurred on April 12, 1994, the day the infamous Canter and Seigel "green card spam" appeared on the Usenet. Their offense was an advertisement posted individually to every Usenet newsgroup, blanketing the whole world with a message advertising their services. At the time, this kind of action was unprecedented and engendered strong disapproval. Not only were most of the audience uninterested in the service, but many people felt that Canter and Seigel had stolen the Usenet's resources. The advertisers did not pay for the transmission of the advertisement; instead the costs were born by the Usenet as a whole.

In the contemporary Internet, spam does not seem surprising; Usenet has largely been given over to it, and ISPs now provide spam filtering services for their users' email both to help their users and in self-defense. Email and Usenet relied on individuals' cooperation to not flood the commons with junk mail, and that cooperation broke down. Today the Internet generally lacks effective technology to prevent spam. The problem is the lack of accountability in the Internet architecture. Because any host can connect to any other host, and because connections are nearly anonymous, people can insert spam into the network at any point. There has been an arms race of trying to hold people accountable—closing down open sendmail relays, tracking sources of spam on Usenet, retaliation against spammers—but the battle has been lost, and today we have all learned to live with spam.

The lesson for peer-to-peer designers is that without accountability in a network, it is difficult to enforce rules of social responsibility. Just like Usenet and email, today's peer-to-peer systems run the risk of being overrun by unsolicited advertisements. It is difficult to design a system where socially inappropriate use is prevented. Technologies for accountability, such as cryptographic identification or reputation systems, can be valuable tools to help manage a peer-to-peer network. There have been proposals to retrofit these capabilities into Usenet and email, but none today are widespread; it is important to build these capabilities into the system from the beginning.

Firewalls, Dynamic IP, NAT

At the same time that the cooperative nature of the Internet was being threatened, network administrators implemented a variety of management measures that resulted in the

Internet being a much less open network. In the early days of the Internet, all hosts were equal participants. The network was symmetric—if a host could reach the Net, everyone on the Net could reach that host. Every computer could equally be a client and a server. This capability began to erode in the mid-1990s with the deployment of firewalls, the rise of dynamic IP addresses, and the popularity of Network Address Translation (NAT). As the Internet matured there came a need to secure the network, to protect individual hosts from unlimited access. By default, any host that can access the Internet can also be accessed on the Internet. Since average users could not handle the security risks that resulted from a symmetric design, network managers turned to firewalls as a tool to control access to their machines.

Firewalls stand at the gateway between the internal network and the Internet outside. They filter packets, choosing which traffic to let through and which to deny. A firewall changes the fundamental Internet model: some parts of the network cannot fully talk to other parts. Firewalls are a very useful security tool, but they pose a serious obstacle to peer-to-peer communication models. A typical firewall works by allowing anyone inside the internal network to initiate a connection to anyone on the Internet, but it prevents random hosts on the Internet from initiating connections to hosts in the internal network.

Allowing an Internet host to be only a client, not a server, is a theme that runs through a lot of the changes in the Internet after the consumer explosion. With the rise of modem users connecting to the Internet, the old practice of giving every Internet host a fixed IP address became impractical, because there were not enough IP addresses to go around. Dynamic IP address assignment is now the norm for many hosts on the Internet, where an individual computer's address may change every single day. Broadband providers are even finding dynamic IP useful for their "always on" services. The end result is that many hosts on the Internet are not easily reachable, because they keep moving around. Peer-to-peer applications such as instant messaging or file sharing have to work hard to circumvent this problem, building dynamic directories of hosts. In the early Internet, where hosts remained static, it was much simpler. A final trend is to not even give a host a valid public Internet address at all, but instead to use NAT to hide the address of a host behind a firewall. NAT combines the problems of firewalls and dynamic IP addresses: not only is the host's true address unstable, it is not even reachable! All communication has to go through a fairly simple pattern that the NAT router can understand, resulting in a great loss of flexibility in applications communications. For example, many cooperative Internet games have trouble with NAT: every player in the game wants to be able to contact every other player, but the packets cannot get through the NAT router. The result is that a central server on the Internet has to act as an application-level message router, emulating the function that TCP/IP itself used to serve.

Firewalls, dynamic IP, and NAT grew out of a clear need in Internet architecture to make scalable, secure systems. They solved the problem of bringing millions of client computers onto the Internet quickly and manageably. But these same technologies have weakened the Internet infrastructure as a whole, relegating most computers to second-class status as clients only. New peer-to-peer applications challenge this architecture, demanding that participants serve resources as well as use them. As peer-to-peer applications become more common, there will be a need for common technical solutions to these problems.

Asymmetric Bandwidth

A final Internet trend of the late 1990s that presents a challenge to peer-to-peer applications is the rise in asymmetric network connections such as ADSL and cable modems. In order to get the most efficiency out of available wiring, current broadband providers have chosen to provide asymmetric bandwidth. A typical ADSL or cable modem installation offers three to eight times more bandwidth when getting data from the Internet than when sending data to it, favoring client over server usage.

The reason this has been tolerated by most users is clear: the Web is the killer app for the Internet, and most users are only clients of the Web, not servers. Even users who publish their own web pages typically do not do so from a home broadband connection, but instead use third-party dedicated servers provided by companies like GeoCities or Exodus. In the early days of the Web it was not clear how this was going to work: could each user have a personal web server? But in the end most Web use is itself asymmetric--many clients, few servers—and most users are well served by asymmetric bandwidth.

The problem today is that peer-to-peer applications are changing the assumption that end users only want to download from the Internet, never upload to it. File-sharing applications such as Napster or Gnutella can reverse the bandwidth usage, making a machine serve many more files than it downloads. The upstream pipe cannot meet demand. Even worse, because of the details of TCP's rate control, if the upstream path is clogged, the downstream performance suffers as well.

So if a computer is serving files on the slow side of a link, it cannot easily download simultaneously on the fast side. ADSL and cable modems assume asymmetric bandwidth for an individual user. This assumption takes hold even more strongly inside ISP networks, which are engineered for bits to flow to the users, not from them. The end result is a network infrastructure that is optimized for computers that are only clients, not servers. But peer-to-peer technology generally makes every host act both as a client and a server; the asymmetric assumption is incorrect. There is not much an individual peer-to-peer application can do to work around asymmetric bandwidth; as peer-to-peer applications become more widespread, the network architecture is going to have to change to better handle the new traffic patterns.

While the new breed of peer-to-peer applications can take lessons from earlier models, these applications also introduce new characteristics or features that are novel. Peer-to-peer allows to separate the concepts of authoring information and publishing that same information. Peer-to-peer allows for decentralized application design, something that is both an opportunity and a challenge. And peer-to-peer applications place unique strains on firewalls, something well demonstrated by the current trend to use the HTTP port for operations other than web transactions.

One of the promises of the Internet is that people are able to be their own publishers, for example, by using personal web sites to make their views and interests known. Self-publishing has certainly become more common with the commercialization of the Internet. More often, however, users spend most of their time reading information and less time publishing, commercial providers of Internet access have structured their offering around this asymmetry. The example of Napster creates an interesting middle ground between the ideal of "everyone publishes" and the seeming reality of "everyone consumes."

Decentralization

Peer-to-peer systems seem to go hand-in-hand with decentralized systems. In a fully decentralized system, not only is every host an equal participant, but there are no hosts with special facilitating or administrative roles. In practice, building fully decentralized systems can be difficult, and many peer-to-peer applications take hybrid approaches to solving problems. As we have already seen,

DNS is peer-to-peer in protocol design but with a built-in sense of hierarchy.

There are many other examples of systems that are peer-to-peer at the core and yet have some semi-centralized organization in application, such as Usenet, instant messaging, and Napster. Usenet is an instructive example of the evolution of a decentralized system. Usenet propagation is symmetric: hosts share traffic. But because of the high cost of keeping a full news feed, in practice there is a backbone of hosts that carry all of the traffic and serve it to a large number of "leaf nodes" whose role is mostly to receive articles. Within Usenet, there was a natural trend toward making traffic propagation hierarchical, even though the underlying protocols do not demand it. This form of "soft centralization" may prove to be economic for many peer-to-peer systems with high-cost data transmission.

Many other current peer-to-peer applications present a decentralized face while relying on a central facilitator to coordinate operations. To a user of an instant messaging system, the application appears peer-to-peer, sending data directly to the friend being messaged. But all major instant messaging systems have some sort of server on the back end that facilitates nodes talking to each other. The server maintains an association between the user's name and his or her current IP address, buffers messages in case the user is offline, and routes messages to users behind firewalls.

Some systems allow direct client-to-client communication when possible but have a server as a fallback. A fully decentralized approach to instant messaging would not work on today's Internet, but there are scaling advantages to allowing client-to-client communication when possible.

Napster is another example of a hybrid system. Napster's file sharing is decentralized: one Napster client downloads a file directly from another Napster client's machine. But the directory of files is centralized, with the Napster servers answering search queries and brokering client connections. This hybrid approach seems to scale well: the directory can be made efficient and uses low bandwidth, and the file sharing can happen on the edges of the network. In practice, some applications might work better with a fully centralized design, not using any peer-to-peer technology at all. One example is a search on a large, relatively static database.

Current web search engines are able to serve up to one billion pages all from a single place. Search algorithms have been highly optimized for centralized operation; there appears to be little benefit to spreading the search operation out on a peer-to-peer network. Also, applications that require centralized information sharing for accountability or correctness are hard to spread out on a decentralized network. Decentralization engenders a whole new area of network-related failures: unreliability, incorrect data synchronization, etc. Peer-to-peer designers need to balance the power of peer-to-peer models against the complications and limitations of decentralized systems.

Abusing port 80

One of the stranger phenomena in the current Internet is the abuse of port 80, the port that HTTP traffic uses when people browse the Web. Firewalls typically filter traffic based on the direction of traffic and the destination port of the traffic. Because the Web is a primary application of many Internet users, almost all firewalls allow outgoing connections on port 80 even if the firewall policy is otherwise very restrictive.

In the early days of the Internet, the port number usually indicated which application was using the network; the firewall could count on port 80 being only for Web traffic. But precisely because many firewalls allow connections to port 80, other application authors started routing traffic through that port. Streaming audio, instant messaging, remote method invocations, even whole mobile agents are being sent through port 80. Most current peer-to-peer applications have some way to use port 80 as well in order to circumvent network security policies. Naive firewalls are none the wiser; they are unaware that they are passing the exact sorts of traffic the network administrator intended to block.

The problem is twofold. First, there is no good way for a firewall to identify what applications are running through it. The port number has already been circumvented. Fancier firewalls can analyze the actual traffic going through the firewall and see if it is a legitimate HTTP stream, but that just encourages application designers to masquerade as HTTP, leading to an escalating arms race that benefits no one.

The second problem is that even if an application has a legitimate reason to go through the firewall, there is no simple way for the application to request permission. The firewall, as a network security measure, is outmoded. As long as a firewall allows some sort of traffic through, peer-to-peer applications will find a way to slip through that opening. The Internet was designed with peer-to-peer applications in mind, but as it has grown the network has become more asymmetric. What can do to permit new peer-to-peer applications to flourish while respecting the pressures that have shaped the Internet to date?

Technical Solutions

The explosion of the Internet into the consumer space brought with it changes that have made it difficult to do peer-to-peer networking. Firewalls make it hard to contact hosts; dynamic IP and NAT make it nearly impossible. Asymmetric bandwidth is holding users back from efficiently serving files on their systems. Current peer-to-peer applications generally would benefit from an Internet more like the original network, where these restrictions were not in place. How can be enable peer-to-peer applications to work better with the current technological situation? Firewalls serve an important need: they allow administrators to express and enforce policies about the use of their networks. That need will not change with peer-to-peer applications. Neither application designers nor network security administrators are benefiting from the current state of affairs.

The solution lies in making firewalls smarter so that peer-to-peer applications can cooperate with the firewall to allow traffic the administrator wants. Firewalls must become more sophisticated, allowing systems behind the firewall to ask permission to run a particular peer-to-peer application. Peer-to-peer designers must contribute to this design discussion, then enable their applications to use these mechanisms. There is a good start to this solution in the SOCKS protocol, but it needs to be expanded to be more flexible and more tied toward applications rather than simple port numbers.

The problems engendered by dynamic IP and NAT already have a technical solution: IPv6. This new version of IP, the next generation Internet protocol architecture, has a 128-bit address space—enough for every host on the Internet to have a permanent address. Eliminating address scarcity means that every host has a home and, in theory, can be reached. The main thing holding up the deployment of IPv6 is the complexity of the changeover. At this stage, it remains to be seen when or even if IPv6 will be commonly deployed, but without it peer-to-peer applications will continue to need to build alternate address spaces to work around the limitations set by NAT and dynamic IP.

Peer-to-peer applications stress the bandwidth usage of the current Internet. First, they break the assumption of asymmetry upon which today's ADSL and cable modem providers rely. There is no simple way that peer-to-peer applications can work around this problem; simply must encourage broadband connections to catch up. However, peer-to-peer applications can do several things to use the existing bandwidth more efficiently. First, data caching is a natural optimization for any peer-to-peer application that is transmitting bulk data; it would be a significant advance to make sure that a program does not have to retransmit or resend data to another host. Caching is a well understood technology: distributed caches like Squid have worked out many of the consistency and load sharing issues that peer-to-peer applications face.

Second, a peer-to-peer application must have effective means for allowing users to control the bandwidth the application uses. Current operating systems and programming libraries do not provide good tools for this kind of limitation, but as peer-to-peer applications start demanding more network resources from hosts, users will need tools to control that resource usage.

Social Solutions

Technical measures can help create better peer-to-peer applications, but good system design can also yield social stability. A key challenge in creating peer-to-peer systems is to have a mechanism of accountability and the enforcement of community standards. Usenet breaks down because it is impossible to hold people accountable for their actions. If a system has a way to identify individuals, that system can be made more secure against antisocial behavior.

Peer-to-peer systems also present the challenge of integrating local administrative control with global system correctness. Usenet was successful at this goal. The local news administrator sets policy for his or her own site, allowing the application to be customized to each user group's needs. The shared communication channel of news.admin allows a community governance procedure for the entire Usenet community. These mechanisms of local and global control were built into Usenet from the beginning, setting the rules of correct behavior. New breed peer-to-peer applications should follow this lead, building in their own social expectations.

The Internet started out as a fully symmetric, peer-to-peer network of cooperating users. As the Net has grown to accommodate the millions of people flocking online, technologies have been put in place that have split the Net up into a system with relatively few servers and many clients. At the same time, some of the basic expectations of cooperation are showing the risk of breaking down, threatening the structure of the Net. These phenomena pose challenges and obstacles to peer-to-peer applications: both the network and the applications have to be designed together to work in tandem. Application authors must design robust applications that can function in the complex Internet environment, and network designers must build in capabilities to handle new peer-to-peer applications. Fortunately, many of these issues are familiar from the experience of the early Internet; the lessons learned there can be brought forward to design tomorrow's systems.

6

Use of New Media in Politics

It seems safe to say that there is a relationship between the application of information and communication technology (ICT) and democracy. For decades now the consequences of ICT for social and political life are disputed in an ideological way. Some call them technologies of freedom, while for others they are technologies of central control and registration. Visions of the rebirth of Athenian democracy are opposed by nightmares of Orwellian proportions.

Others again, stress the ambiguity of this technology which is enabling as well as defining and leaves opportunities of choice within certain limits. These are theoretical interpretations of the use of ICT which existed before it was practised on a large scale. In the meantime ICT has massively entered organisations, among them political, government and administrative organisations. The effects of ICT on the practice of these organisations can not be denied any more. The interpretations of the meaning of ICT can be specified now and released from some of the early speculations.

This chapter is about the positive contribution of the use of ICT to the political system in general and political democracy in particular. It deals with several directions of improvement guided by different conceptions of democracy. This does not mean that negative effects of the use of ICT for the political system and democracy, lightly touched upon in the former paragraph, can be ruled out in advance. People who conceive ICT as a technology of central control and registration will not perceive any beneficial effects for democracy and reject particular views of the renewal of democracy, such as notions of direct democracy, as utopian or dangerous views. They tend to think that the best thing which can happen is a preservation of the current political system and the present quality of democracy. One type of analysis can not be ignored. Several analysts argue that the field of democracy itself is losing ground together with the declining influence of the political system of the nation state.

This is a type of rule by the fragmented global political power of transnational corporations and other organisations who, like feudal lords, surpass the nation states and undermine their power to take or implement decisions. All kinds of national and international organisations are filling the vacuum and creating undemocratic or uncontrollable types of political power by means of information and communication networks, informal social networks, corruption and even crime.

The democracy within transnational corporations and other global associations is at a far lower level than the democracy of national institutional politics. The power of a European parliament or a United Nations does not match the present power of the nation states with a democratic rule either. The analysis of the decline of the nation state by some other social or political scientists is less dramatic. The political primacy of the nationstate and institutional politics are questioned, not democracy in its own right. Other places and ways of democracy in civil society can replace or add to the institutional democracy of the nation state. This position at least can be located in one of the positive models of democracy to be dealt with now.

Models of Democracy

From the first introduction of the new information and communication technologies, marked by the design and diffusion of interactive and integrative multimedia, these technologies appeared to be connected to conceptions of democracy. The new facilities of telepolling, telereferenda and electronic elections immediately spurred visions of there birth of the Athenian agora and other means of direct democracy and self-representation. These visions were rejected with equal vigour by defenders of an improved representative system and people who were very sceptic about "push- button democracy".

The opportunities of the new media for direct or representative democracy has lingered for about twenty years. In these decades two things appeared. First, the conceptions of democracy are much more complicated than a simple dualism between direct and representative democracy. Second, discussions have become less theoretical; the media of ICT are maturing and entering into the daily practice of the political system. One can observe stages of experimentation and beyond.

So we will have to do two things, elaborate the conceptions of democracy connected to the practice of ICT and describe this practice with regard to its introduction in the political system. Still we hope to show in a plausible way that some typical views of democracy are connected to particular practices of ICT in politics. This goes as far as the suggestion of a relationship of these views with concrete instruments of ICT in the political system like computerised citizen enquiries, opinion polls, referend a, public information systems, government information and registration systems, electronic town halls and free nets (Table 1).

Table 1: Electronic instruments of politics and democracy arranged according to information traffic patterns

---

Allocution
- computerised election campaigns
- computerised information campaigns
- civic service and information centres

Consultation
- mass public information systems
- advanced public information systems (the Internet, etc.)

Registration
- registration systems for government and public -administration
- computer-assisted citizen enquiries
- electronic polls
- electronic referenda
- electronic elections

Conversation
- bulletin board systems
- discussion lists
- electronic mail and teleconferencing
- electronic town halls
- group decision support systems

Sometimes these views are very explicit, as in the conception of direct democracy mentioned above. More often they remain implicit. In this chapter they are made explicit for the purposes of clarification and explanation. There is not much to prove yet at this stage of introduction of ICT into the political system. The large number of conceptions of democracy can only be summarised by analytical means. A successful attempt to do this has been made by David Held in his Models of democracy. Held constructs nine models in the history of democracy. A model is "a theoretical construction designed to reveal and explain the chief elements of democratic form and its underlying structure and relations". He distinguishes four classical and five contemporary models.

The classical models are classical democracy, protective democracy, developmental democracy and direct democracy. The contemporary models are competitive-elitist democracy, pluralism, legal democracy, participatory democracy and developmental autonomy. The first four of these models will be used in this chapter. We have clearly observed views belonging to them in the design and use of ICT in politics. This is not the case with the last model, developmental autonomy, which seems first of all the favourite model of Held himself. Instead of this model add a fifth one which is based upon direct democracy. It is clearly present in some designs and uses of ICT in politics. We will call it plebiscitary democracy.

Held's analysis can be elaborated and improved by the construction of an analytical space relating the five selected models of democracy. Two dimensions typify the differences in the present views of democracy: what should be the goals and the means of democracy? Should its prime goal be opinion formation or decision making? In other words, is democracy primarily a matter of substantial input or of procedure (an output)? Should these goals be reached first of all by the ways of representative or direct democracy? The selected models of democracy can be located in a two-dimensional analytical space.

Information and communication technology offers means first of all. So it seems most interesting to find out which means are favoured in the design and use of this technology in the political system. In Table 1 a spectrumis drawn of representative and direct means which will be described in the next sections. ICT can be used to reinforce the present, mainly representative political system to confront its difficulties mentioned in the introduction and to rescue or revive the primacy of institutional politics.

ICT can also be used to displace politics on to civil society by means of participation, pluralism and direct citizen power, abandoning the attempts to save the present political system attached to the nationstate in crisis and removing the political primacy, at least partially, to the associations and individuals of civil society. With the aid of ICT, politics can be moved to the market as well. In this case the freedom of choice of producers and consumers is made equal to the vote of citizens. ICT is treated as a technology of freedom offering ways of decision making which can replace traditional ways of political decision making.

It is very important to realise that these models are theoretical constructions. In fact they are ideal types. In the reality of political systems and views several of them can be combined, often in contradictory ways. For instance, the political system of the United States is a combination of a legalist model, a competitive model, a plebiscitary model and a pluralist model. Still, these models describe real institutions, conceptions and differences of opinion, as hope to show in the next five sections.

Legalist Democracy

The first model is based on the classical Western conception of democracy which came into being after the decline of the absolutist state in Western Europe. It is reflected in most contemporary constitutions. The first advocates of the legalist model were Locke and Montesquieu. It is called legalist as it clearly is a procedural conception which takes the constitution and the law as the basis of democracy.

According to most contemporary constitutions state authority is separated into three powers controlled by a system of checks and balances. Another important principle is majority rule. This rule is taken to be universal except for particular basic rights of the individual which are also part of the constitution. In the legalist model, democracy is a means to safeguard the freedom of individuals from authoritarian power. It is not a goal in its own right.

A system of representation is proposed. The heart of political system is the judgement of heterogeneous interests and complex problems by representatives of the people. Direct democracy is rejected. Populism is feared. The power of every political institution and public administration has to be limited by the least possible, but effective rules. The system of politics and public administration has to be small and effective. For this reason the legalist model is very popular among conservatives and liberals.

The basic assumption in this model with regard to the meaning of ICT for the political system is that it should solve its basic problem: information shortage. The present crisis of the political system and the nation state is viewed as the crisis of organisations which can not sufficiently deal with the increasing complexity of the environment and the system itself, as information is lacking, among others by the obstructions caused by bureaucracy. The so-called gap between governors or administrators and citizens is also conceived as a kind of information shortage on both sides.

Finally, all kinds of threats to the separation of powers, and checks and balances in the system, most often caused by the rising power of the executive as compared to the legislative state, are accounted to deficiencies of information as well. It is a matter of sharing the power of information. The problem can be solved by an equal supply of the resources of information to the executive and to parliaments, municipal councils, political parties and other representatives.

So, following the legalist model ICT is designed and used as a means to remove information shortages and reinforce the present political system by more effective and efficient ways of information processing and organisation. ICT is also applied to increase the transparency of the political system. By all these means the system would be capable to confront the problems of complexity. For some proponents of the legalist model, usually not the conservative or liberal ones, this means a revival of the steering ambition of the state, so much discredited in the 1980s.

Which are the favourite media or instruments of ICT following this model of democracy? The chosen instruments should serve two functions. First, they would have to supply more and better information to governors, administrators, representatives and citizens. Second, the interactive communication capacities of the new media might create a representative government which is more open and responsive to the people, not directly controlled by the people. Both functions can only be fulfilled by instruments of ICT under the control of governors, administrators and representatives.

In Table 1 they can by found under the headings of allocution, consultation and registration. The preferred instruments are computerised information campaigns, civic service and information centres, mass public information systems, registration systems for the government and the public administration and computer assisted citizen enquiries. Registration and conversation media such as electronic polls or referenda and electronic debates between citizens are not adopted at all. They are deeply distrusted.

Competitive Democracy

The second model of democracy is also based on aprocedural view of representative democracy. Elections of representatives are considered to be the most important operations of the political system. The advocates of this model strongly reject the possibility of direct democracy. According to the best-known designers of this model, Max Weber and Joseph Schumpeter, direct democracy is impossible in large, complex and heterogeneous societies.

A central role for bureaucracy, political parties and leaders with authority is inevitable. Politics has to be seen as an everlasting competition between parties and their leaders for the support of the voting public. In this way the best leaders and representatives are elected. This is the solution for the problems of complexity and the crisis of the political system. It is also the main difference as compared to the legalist model which is based on a balance of executive and legislative power and on responsive representation.

In the competitive model power is entrusted to leaders and experts in the executive power. They rule the apparatus of state, they weigh matters and interests against each other, they solve conflicts with negotiations and they command authority.. As leadership is emphasised in this model, it is called competitive-elitist by Held. Inone respect this is not a good label for it: populism is one of the best-known electoral strategies in this model.

The competitive model is practised first of all in presidential states and two-party political systems. It is gaining popularity in contemporary politics as the role of persons and personalities in politics grows. This role was reinforced by old media such as television and will best rengthened even further by the audio-visual new media enabling all kinds of techniques in direct mail, marketing, targeting and visual manipulation.

The last-called facilities show the way to the design and use of ICT in politics according to this model. First of all, ICT will be used in election and information campaigns. The voting public will be reached by a combination of television and interactive media which serve as direct channels to target a selective audience of potential voters with differentiated political messages. In the second place, the interested public, the fragmented electoral base of political leaders and parties should have the opportunity to get information about views, stands and voting behaviour of their leaders and representatives. So they need access to mass and advanced public information systems.

Finally, the registration systems of the government and the public administration are vital to a strong and efficient state authority. Other means of registration and conversation, such as electronic polls and town halls, are only used for the benefit of the political leadership. Their resemblance to direct democracy is deceptive.

Plebiscitary Democracy

The design and use of direct channels of communication between the political leaders and the citizenry can be transformed into an altogether different view of politics and democracy. In this case these channels are not used to strengthen the position of governors, politicians and administrators, but to amplify the voice of the citizenry. This is the central tenet of the plebiscitarian model of democracy. It is based on notions of direct democracy as away of decision making.

The essential difference with the competitive and legalist models is the displacement of politics from the government and the administration on to society and the world of the individual citizen in particular. According to the plebiscitarian views the decisions in the political system should be taken by as was possible representatives and as much as possible by individual citizens by means of plebiscites.

The advent of ICT and the new interactive media stimulated a renaissance of plebliscitarian views in the United States from the 1,960s onwards. The concept of teledemocracy was invented. Many local experiments have been waged. In these experiments old and new media were redesigned and used to open channels between the local government or administration and individual citizens. Well-known American experimenters were Becker and Barber. They set their hopes on the technical capacities of the new media. They would be able to remove the age-old practical barriers of direct democracy in a large, complex society.

The political primacy of the government and institutional politics, already in a state of crisis, would not have to be saved. Apolitical system based on a continuing registration of the peoples will and, for some advocates, the will of consumers on the market as well, might be able to replace this role and this primacy.

Following the plebiscitarian model the logical preferences in ICT are registration systems of the votes and opinions of citizens. Telepolls, telereferenda and televotes by means of telephone and computer networks, two way cable television or future information highways are the favourite instruments. As a well-known criticism of this conception of democracy points at its individualisation and atomisation of the citizenry and its simplification of issues, instruments of conversation are added sometimes. This means the design of electronic town halls, teleconferencing and other new discussion channels. Of course, instruments of consultation by citizens themselves, mass and advanced public information systems, can not be discarded either. However, all instruments filled with information by institutional politics are distrusted.

Pluralist Democracy

In the competitive, legalist and plebiscitarian models of democracy nothing seems to exist between the state and the representation on the one hand and the individual citizen on the other. In the pluralist model, to the contrary, attention is called to the role of the intermediary organisations and associations of civil society. Alex is de Tocqueville observed the conspicuous role of these organisations in the American democracy of the eighteenth century. A network conception of politics is favoured as opposed to the centralist views of the legalist model and the elitist competitive model.

The present decline of the central nation state and the displacement of politics is not deplored. On the contrary, it is acclaimed. In the pluralist model, democracy is not the sovereign power of the majority but an always shifting coalition of minorities. The state should act as an arbiter. If it is supposed to put the different parties in an equal position by some kind of social policy, a progressive type of pluralist democracy. If it is supposed to refrain from doing this, meet a liberal or conservative type of it. So, the pluralist model is a combination of direct and representative democracy. Representation is made continually, not only by professional politicians selected every four or five years, but by all kinds of organisational representatives as well.

The constitutional state can be accepted, but its real substance and resources are produced by the intermediary organisations of civil society. In Western Europe the most frequent result was some kind of corporatist state. The words" substance" and "resource" indicate that substantial democracy is preferred to a procedural conception of it. Ultimately, opinion formation in civil society, based on interests is more important for democracy than decision making in the central state.

Two characteristics of the new media in ICT are very attractive to this model of democracy. First, the multiplication of channels and stand-alone media supports the potential pluriformity of political information. Every view and every organisation or association can have its say. They can reach their own and every other interested audience. Second, the advance of interactive communication networks, in contrast to the allocution of broadcasting, perfectly fits to a network conception of politics.

Following these two general preferences, all instruments or systems which can be used to reinforce information and communication inside the organisations of civil society or between them will be favoured. These are most instruments arranged under the patterns of consultation, registration and conversation in Table 1. This time these instruments are used, first of all, by the organisations of civil society to inform and register their membership and external audiences. They are mass and advanced public information systems, registration systems. However, the most favourite instruments to a pluralist model of democracy are conversation systems inside or among organisations, associations and individual citizens: electronic mail, discussion lists, teleconferencing and decision support systems for the most complex problems.

Participatory Democracy

The last model of democracy to be described is close to the pluralist model in several aspects. It is a combination of representative and direct democracy. It is based on views of democracy emphasising the substantial aspects and resources of democracy even more than the pluralist model. The big difference is the shift in attention from organisations to citizens. The support of citizenship is the central aim in the model of participatory democracy.

Jean Jeacques Rousseau is the first classical advocate of this model. He can be considered a proponent of direct democracy, but not in its plebiscitarian brand. Rousseau's notion of the people's will is not based upon the measurement of the views of individual citizens, but it aims at the development of citizenship by means of collective discussion and education. Educating citizens as active members of the community is the primary aim in this model which clearly originates in the Enlightenment. For Rousseau, the people's will was not a sum of individual wills but some kind of totality revealing the sovereignty of the people as a collective. This totality had to be created in public meetings and legislative assemblies. One of the latter-day interpretations was the council or Soviet type of democracy covering a large part of the Marxist tradition; in its practice this totality was often transformed into talitarianism.

A necessary condition of this model of democracy is the presence of informed citizens. The centres of political power themselves should become more accessible to citizens. They should be responsive to their questions and certainly not only pose questions to them. The individualist bias of the plebiscitarian and competitive views is firmly opposed. Plebiscites, electronic or otherwise, are feared for the isolation of the individual citizen and the possibility of central manipulation.

Another threat is a separation of opinion polling and opinion formation. Polling in its own right is considered to be a poor and passive type of political participation directed by simple and prefabricated questions. A complete fragmentation of political practiceis expected; collective opinion formation in discussions and educational contexts is preferred.

The logical consequence of this model of democracy is the option of instruments of ICT which are able to inform and activate the citizenry. Computerised information campaigns and mass public information systems have to be designed and supported in such a way that they help to narrow the gap between the "information rich" and the "information poor," otherwise the spontaneous development of ICT will widen it. Therefore the access and the user friendliness of the new media should be improved. According to the participatory view this is the only way to really open or make transparent the political system to the mass of the citizenry.

The electronic instruments of discussion are taken as a second option. They are attractive as they could be means for opinion formation, learning and active participation.

Discussion lists on public computer networks, teleconferences and electronic town halls might be very useful. However, a first condition is that not only the social and intellectual elite will participate in them. A second one is their design as suitable instruments of discussion. Both conditions are badly fulfilled at this moment. The socalled virtual communities created on the Internet and other public networks are extremely overpopulated by male, affluent people with high education. The quality of the discussions in these networks is rather low, as some communication capacities of these new media do not support fruitful discussion.

The elaboration of five contemporary models of democracy was made to suggest that the goals and means of designing and using ICT in the political system can be very different. The same goes for the promotion of democracy within this system. It makes a difference whether the primary goal of democracy is opinion or decision making. These goals could be reconciled in practice as some electronic instruments used in politics and for the benefit of democracy are able to serve both aims, for instance computer-assisted citizen enquiries, electronic mail and teleconferencing, electronic town halls, and group decision support systems. To reconcile the different means of democracy is a much more difficult matter.

As general models representative and direct democracy are fundamentally opposed. As any one knows, the results of referenda often disturb and contradict the decision-making process in the representative system. This is why these direct instruments should remain subordinate to the workings of the representative system of democracy according to the advocates of this system.

On the other hand it is possible, and presumably necessary in practice, to insert some kind of representation in a working system of direct democracy. However, a fundamental problem is that a system of daily telepolls, referenda, tele-elections and electronic debates would undermine the authority of every representative and parliament continually. The advocates of the models of democracy can not be solved. Only compromises can be made.

Of course they really are made in daily political practice. However, often these compromises are uneasy and contradictory ones. These kinds of compromises are most likely to increase in the design and application of ICT in politics and democracy. In practice the results often are unclear definitions of the goals of experiments with ICT in politics or they are a compromise of a multitude of very different, even contradictory goals.

7

Internet Communication and Social Development

Improved communication and information access are directly related to social and economic development. The Internet is a multipurpose tool, a medium of communication and perhaps the most flexible medium currently available. It has the potential to be integrated within a wide variety of efforts that have objectives such as local participation, training, education, research, technical support and institutional strengthening. Thus, endeavours that might find a role for Internet applications could range from training to the development of criteria and indicators for sustainable agriculture.

The Internet today is a people's network. Anyone with basic computer equipment and a telephone line can connect to it, communicate through it, host information on it and look through or browse it. Unlike many other media such as television and radio, every user of the medium can be an information producer and knowledge sharer. Communicating over the Internet costs a fraction of what it does to use traditional telephones or fax because information flows in discrete packets of digital bits that are able to share telecommunication lines with hundreds of other packets.

Where a traditional transatlantic telephone call will tie up a single telephone line for only two people, an e-mail message can travel along a telephone line with hundreds and even thousands of other messages. A fact that is well known to veteran Internet users is that the Internet has the power to cut across social and geographic distance and help people find new ways of facilitating the flow of information and knowledge.

With regard to Internet use in support of rural and agricultural development, applications fall into five main areas: economic development for agricultural producers, community development, research/education, SME development and media networks. Rural communities and small-scale agricultural producers are deeply affected by global economic, environmental and political forces. The idea that communities of small-scale agricultural producers are isolated and living in closed, self-sufficient societies is a myth. In fact, with the appropriate knowledge, small-scale producers can even have a competitive edge over larger operations.

When knowledge is harnessed by strong organizations of small producers, strategic planning can be used to provide members with lower-cost inputs, better storage facilities, improved transportation links and collective negotiations with buyers. The Internet is one tool that can enhance this flow of information. It is an inexpensive way to communicate and access global information. Local Internet services can be easily managed by well-organized local user groups and farmers' organizations. Information and analyses can be tailored to local, regional and national knowledge and communication needs and realities. When combined with national and global market information systems, and with the ability to communicate quickly with potential buyers and brokers, local Internet systems become valuable strategic planning and decision-making tools.

Community information centres and farmers' organizations can also gather information from the Internet and disseminate it via local radio stations, newspapers and other local information-sharing networks and tools. For example, daily market prices and agricultural news can be posted at cooperatives, local stores, transportation hubs, agricultural supply outlets and social gathering points. Simple newsletters can be developed using Internet information and distributed to members of farmers' organizations. When integrated with other media tools, the Internet can be a powerful information resource and research tool. Internet services are also valuable when placed at the service of rural development-oriented organizations which act as local communication conduits or intermediaries. Along with providing improved market knowledge, they can also:

— develop locally appropriate applications and creative services;

— provide knowledge about successful development strategies;

— enable efficient regional, national and global organizational efforts .

— improve access to a huge variety of information, training, research and educational resources (including distance education services) which are typically unavailable in rural and remote areas because of the costs associated with printed materials and books;

— enable rural young people to learn about computers and to have access to the technologies and information available to their urban peers;

— provide access to critical technical information for rural professionals such as physicians, health care workers, technicians and engineers, thereby providing further encouragement for these professionals to continue practising in rural and remote communities;

— be used as marketing tools to promote rural tourism and market the products of small secondary industries and home-based businesses;

— enable local NGOs to gain a global presence and make better contact with potential donors and supporters through the on-line publication of resources and information and through the use of electronic mail; and

— sensitize urban policy-makers to the realities and needs of rural populations.

Internet use among intermediary organizations and leaders involved in participatory research can provide a cost-effective method for documenting and sharing lessons learned and research results. Internet use also has the potential to strengthen linkages between and among farmers' organizations, extension workers, researchers and policy-makers. The cost of accessing printed academic materials within developing countries is usually so high that students and faculty members have great difficulty acquiring books and journals. Furthermore, the time required to obtain printed materials from overseas can be long enough to render some information outdated by the time it arrives. Via the Internet, any information published on-line can be accessed almost instantly and at a fraction of the cost of obtaining printed materials. Archival lists of resources can be easily reviewed and assessed in remote locations. With the assistance of Internet tools, these partnerships can be further strengthened and Internet learning resources can be cooperatively developed across oceans to be utilized by participants in developing nations. Overall, the Internet holds significant potential to enhance learning and research relationships among researchers, academics and students wherever they may be located. The list of potential applications is infinite and thousands of informal linkages of this sort take place every day in Internet discussion groups.

Development of Internet Applications

The news media in developing countries have also been at the forefront of developing Internet applications. In addition to the latter news and information applications, organizations such as Inter Press Service (IPS) Third World News Agency use the Internet to source news stories from local writers in developing countries and share those stories with international wire services such as Associated Press. IPS is also able to provide Internet feeds that enable African news media to have access to African news from around the continent. his is particularly relevant to rural radio stations and other rural newspaper and newsletter producers that would otherwise be unable to obtain the same news from other sources.

IPS can also provide an outlet for rural news writers to share their stories regionally, nationally and globally. Similar Internet strategies for rural radio networks, which might also incorporate digital audio transmissions, may well emerge in the near future.The Internet is not a panacea for rural development, but it does bring new information resources and can open new communication channels for rural communities. It offers a means for bridging the gaps between development professionals and rural people by initiating interaction and dialogue, new alliances, interpersonal networks and cross-sectoral links between organizations. It can create mechanisms that enable the bottom-up articulation and sharing of local knowledge. Benefits include increased efficiency in the use of development resources, less duplication of activities, reduced communication costs and global access to information and human resources.

The Internet may help in meeting peoples' information and communication objectives in order to attain their development goals and objectives, but it must be integrated within human contexts and seen as a "communication process tool", not simply a static "information technology" or unit-directional broadcast medium. Otherwise, Internet tools will be relegated to the junk heaps of inappropriate development technologies or dismissed because of previous failures to make the medium locally relevant and useful. Of course, the Internet is not the only communications tool that may be used; radio and television may have equal or even greater potential, at least for the moment. We must avoid contributing to the gap between the information haves and the information have-nots that can emerge when we create Internet applications to serve only privileged researchers and bureaucrats. In particular, we must strive to find ways to bring knowledge producers, such as researchers and policy-makers, closer to the other less recognized knowledge producers: the people who are the ultimate beneficiaries of their development programmes.

Early Internet users in developing countries have proved that they can develop excellent local services and locally appropriate knowledge resources. However, without support from development agencies, there is a risk that such efforts will never meet the needs of people in rural communities. Adopting a proactive strategy and acting to bring the Internet to rural and agricultural communities in developing countries will help enable rural people to face the unprecedented challenges brought on by the changing global economy, political changes, environmental degradation and demographic pressures. To deal with these challenges and to make critical decisions, people at all levels of society, and especially the food-insecure and the organizations that serve and represent them, must be able to access critical information and communicate. The time to act in support of Internet knowledge and communication systems in developing countries is now. Today we truly live in a global village, but it is a village with privileged "information haves" and many "information have-nots".

Participatory approaches

Electronic communication networks (ECNs) can be used to promote participatory exchange of information, knowledge and experiences at the grass roots level. ECN is a new medium of communication, and its casting and content need to be thought through. Participatory approaches can help in ECN design and use by all involved. Before looking at the details of why and how there could be benefits, it is important for us to understand what we mean by "participatory approaches". There are many forms of participation, but the bottom line is that communities participate genuinely if they will derive benefits aimed at satisfying their real felt needs as they define them themselves. These benefits need not solely be material benefits - material benefits only make sense when they satisfy communities' fundamental needs such as subsistence, identity, freedom, protection, affection, understanding, participation, creation and leisure.

If participation is a basic need, it is worth looking at the typology of different types of participation so as to put the type of participation that empowers communities in the context of other non-genuine forms of participation. Structurally, villagers should have an understanding of the systems involved. They need to understand the system of networking they are involved in. This is important if they are to be empowered to get maximum benefit out of the system. Like designing any communication programme, and the communication media and activities that go with it, designing an ECN has several challenges if it is done in a participatory manner:

— how to design the system properly through research of the needs of key interaction groups including rural groups, the community, change agents, or facilitators if involved; and

— how to design the system properly through a participatory design process.

Such assessment would focus on issues such as:

— segmentation of interaction groups by such factors as gender, age groups, occupation, wealth, etc.;

— content identification;

— subjects and purpose, for example, for awareness, entertainment or training;

— packaging of the interface and the content;

— using visuals or audio-visuals to assist overcoming gaps of literacy; and

— activities that encourage responses.

Some ECN materials may need to be tailored to specific audiences, but this does not preclude connection to the Internet although it focuses on immediate needs for purposes of encouraging participation and developmental objectives. A major issue is how the system will be designed to bridge the first mile with participatory approaches that use other media and channels to encourage people's inputting and receiving relevant information, knowledge and experiences to and from the network, even though they do not have direct access to the computer.

Through participatory rural communication appraisal, establish how 'a' wants communication coming from 'b', 'c', 'd', or 'e', to be packaged when it is received and the type of information wanted from each different point. The reverse is equally true; that is, each point can establish how 'a' can send particular types of information they need in terms of packaging.

Electronic communication networking could easily supercharge the speed of everything from cash flow to customer services in a community. The network in this case is not only a means of facilitating business but the business itself. Since important activities cannot be entrusted to one person, the community will need to be organized/ reorganized to deal with the new changes in communication. Changes in communication of this nature bring extreme changes like free-flowing information, and the community needs to be organised for this. Information is power, and investing it in few hands could disempower the other villagers. This can be overcome by group rather than individual training.

Village activities are usually conducted under a big tree or in a big grass thatched enclosure with the people sitting together, circular fashion that is intimate. Information received (e.g., for training, marketing, inputs, prices, etc.) could be enlarged from a PC monitor to an overhead projector screen and the villagers could together or in groups discuss and strategize on what action to take next. As soon as they make their decision they could respond via the same medium. Juxtaposed to this is the possibility of the extension worker, the facilitator at village level, being an information worker too. This means people can still meet under the big tree or big grass thatched hut and discuss information they have received and plan together sending back replies. However, the information worker will also play the role of decoding a lot of information, which could be difficult to comprehend or respond to. Although emphasis is placed on group activity, we should not make it seem a must. Whereas in nascent community organizations group approaches are strong, in emergent and mature community organization decisions taken collectively are more and more delegated to individuals to implement or critique.

If people cannot read and write it is not the end of the world. Programmes can be designed so that people understand interaction in the written word with regards to specific functions. This has been known to work very well with teaching bookkeeping to village groups involved in small-scale enterprises.

Villagers are not concerned about into food security only. A resource such as electronic communication network would be under-utilised if left for one function only. The people may like such a resource to be linked to development of other things like a library, information on opportunities for school leavers and entertainment. Participatory approaches could also establish different preferred information and communication needs. The systems, the technology itself and the atmosphere should be sensitive to the needs of women, men, children, adults and old people. If conflicts arise in use or content or type of technology, villagers would need to be familiar with conflict mediation and resolution.

Internet Connectivity on Rural Areas

The impacts of non-governmental organizations with Internet connectivity on rural communities represents an attempt to address the shortcomings of previous ICT evaluations. It is not meant to be a definitive study of how to examine rural communities' information sharing with NGOs possessing Internet connectivity, but it does propose a framework from which to build upon, improve, and make as relevant as possible an understanding of the benefits and impacts of the Internet for those who lack connectivity in rural areas of developing countries. Only through application in the field can such frameworks be tested, assessed, and improved upon. It is hoped that this framework represents a fresh approach to understanding the complex issues and networks involved in information sharing and ICT use.

Much of the literature on the use of information and communication technologies (ICT) concerns the potential that such investments offer for the developing world. Yet despite the rhetoric of how ICT can bridge the gap between the information haves and the have-nots, there is little research available that demonstrates that the use of ICT are in fact able to bridge that gap. Moreover, the focus of ICT research is currently fixated on the institutional level, which is composed of Internet service providers (ISPs), policy makers and governments. While the value of such research is not challenged here, the fact remains that very little investigation has been conducted concerning the impacts of ICT on those who have the most to gain through the expansion of ICT in the developing world: the rural stakeholder communities.

The benefits of expanding ICT to major urban cities has been well-documented, and the results of such urban investment can be seen in both the expansion of ISPs and the increasing connectivity throughout the cities of the developing world. Furthermore, the economics involved in development agencies' and corporations' willingness to expand Internet connectivity into rural areas in both Northern and Southern hemispheres has proven to be a major stumbling block. In fact, rather than expansion being based upon the desire to meet the communication needs of rural communities, rural ICT expansion is primarily based on the degree to which it will be a profitable and worthwhile venture for the communication companies involved.

The exclusion of rural communities and stakeholders from ICT expansion occurs in spite of the benefits that ICT is intended to bring to the isolated areas of the world. Even with the inclusion of the two questions relating to local stakeholders' acceptance, support, and ability to assume ownership of ICT, the CIDA report offers vague, insufficient analysis of the rural impacts of ICT. This is evidenced in the presentation of a case study of a Peruvian rural telephone expansion project; the report states that the project's immediate impact is an increase in telecommunications access for 200 000 people. Beyond this statistic, however, the report was unable to identify any of the direct and indirect impacts of this project at the community level.

There is a need to refocus ICT research so that the communication processes occurring with the use of the Internet are examined, rather than the infrastructural components themselves. Through learning how communities without Internet connectivity are able to benefit from organizations that have connectivity, and through learning how the two entities can work together to ensure that information is received, shared, and put to good use, those in development can move towards guaranteeing that stakeholders' needs are being met, and that adequate support is provided to those who need it most. If the benefits of the Internet are not made available to the rural peoples who can benefit from it the most, "then we are failing to fully leverage the large infrastructure investments involved, and we are failing to assist people in making appropriate decisions based on such valuable information".

The concept of participatory development communication is central to examining the use of the Internet as it relates to rural community stakeholders. Its basic tenet is that, "the communication process is more important than the production of media products". Participatory communication for development is a process that emphasizes a two-way communication process based on sharing ideas and information in order to improve the quality of life of the stakeholder communities. Unlike traditional com-munication methods of disseminating and transmitting information, development for communication "is about aiding different types of actors interested in understanding needs and assessing opportunities jointly; it is about providing them with the methods and media to reach common meaning, and about enabling them to negotiate with other actors with contrasting perceptions and interests".

The Internet is the latest in a long line of communication tools that enable a community to receive information and assistance from outside organizations. Unlike technologies such as radio, newspaper, and video, however, the Internet, "is the first media tool that allows every user to be a sender, receiver, narrowcaster and broadcaster". The tremendous opportunities that such technology can offer to rural stakeholder communities must not be missed. The challenge, however, is ensuring that the Internet is utilized for two-way communication processes such as communicating local knowledge and perceptions.

Current evaluations tend to ignore those rural stakeholders who are without connectivity. The need exists for an evaluation approach that will specifically examine the impacts of ICT on development at a grassroots level. Michel Menou writes of the importance of understanding the grassroots' impacts from the Internet when he states that "lower level data are needed to interpret higher trends". He goes further in suggesting the importance of focusing on this segment of the population when discussing the issue of equality of access to information. Such access, "must also be considered in relation to its effectiveness for the worst-off segments of the population, such as handicapped people or geographically scattered rural populations. The time to focus on the processes that accompany technological tools such as the Internet is now.

Without understanding how ICT such as the Internet are impacting those at the grassroots level, we risk remaining unaware of the effectiveness of technological investments that occur at the institutional level. The Internet is not a panacea for rural and agricultural development, but it does bring new information resources and can open up new communication channels for rural communities and agricultural organizations. It offers a means for bridging the gaps between development professionals, rural people and agricultural producers through the initiation of interaction and dialogue. It can foster new alliances and interpersonal networks together with lateral and cross-sector links between organizations.

Most importantly, it can support mechanisms that enable the bottom-up articulation and sharing of information on needs and local knowledge. Primary benefits include increased efficiency in the use of development resources, less duplication of activities, reduced communication costs and global access to information and human resources. None of these benefits are guaranteed by the technology of the Internet. Instead, they are realized when people work together to make the most of a decentralized and accessible communication tool. There has been a rapid increase in the use of the Internet in developing countries. With regard to rural and agricultural development and the Internet, organizations that support the betterment of rural populations and improvements in agriculture have important roles to play.

For example, the Food and Agriculture Organization of the United Nations, is playing an important role in assisting the establishment and growth of Internet services for rural communities and for agricultural development. In partnership with local stakeholders and other development agencies, organizations like FAO can help rural communities and agricultural organizations realize the benefits of improved communication and access to information.

Enormous benefits await rural communities and agricultural organizations when communication improves between the non-governmental organizations, government services, private sector entities and educational institutes that support rural and agricultural development. By sharing information about their activities in the fields of agriculture, rural development, forestry, fisheries, health, nutrition, and education, these agencies can better serve rural people and farmers. They can make use of "lessons learned," determine and use "best practices," and coordinate information about particular regions or successful development approaches. At the same time, rural communities and agricultural organizations can benefit equally from improved vertical channels of communication that enable rural stakeholders and farmers to communicate with decision-makers and others concerned with development.

An integrated approach to the expansion of Internet services will promote the necessary (but often neglected) horizontal communication between agencies linked to rural and agricultural development. At the same time, an integrated approach will provide the tools to enable rural people and farmers to enter directly into new vertical communication relationships with external agencies. Improving horizontal communication can improve the quality and relevance of information resources and and physical resources available to rural people. Improving vertical communication between rural people, farmers and decision-makers can improve the quality of decisions that affect rural communities and agricultural organizations.

An integrated approach provides for vertical communication by establishing rural Internet access sites, and by enhancing horizontal communication between such entities as agricultural colleges, agricultural input and equipment suppliers, government extension services, rural development organizations, health care agencies, and agricultural research and documentation centres. Improved horizontal communication can also include existing media services that serve rural stakeholders. For example, throughout the developing world, rural radio and, increasingly, television broadcast services, are important information delivery mechanisms. Their services improve significantly through the exchange of information and news by way of the Internet. African news items are commonly circulated among African news agencies via the Internet.

Rural African radio stations are able to take advantage of Internet services to provide extension and rural development information from qualified research sources from around the world. Internet services, in conjunction with existing and more widely used communication media such as rural radio, will enable the broadest enhancement of information and communication resources for rural people. For example, national or regional agricultural market information systems or extension information systems hosted on the Internet can be excellent information sources for the staff of rural radio stations throughout a region or nation.

Using information on current market prices broadcast by rural radio stations, farmers can negotiate better prices from local buyers. Improved horizontal communication and improved information resources can improve the quality of the decisions and interventions that impact upon rural people. At the same time, these improvements can enhance rural peoples' direct participation in development. Establishing rural Internet access sites and facilities in concert with efforts to enhance horizontal communication networks among the agencies involved in rural and agricultural development is the essence of the integrated approach highlighted.

Sustainabile Development

Current evidence suggests that to achieve sustainability and success, Internet projects for rural and agricultural development must begin with the real needs of the local community of users. This requires an approach that catalyzes local participation, supports information and communication needs assessments, creates awareness of potential Internet uses, helps build communities of users, and facilitates locally managed, self-supporting communication and information networks. It also requires attention to capacity building and institutional strengthening for the intermediary agencies that serve rural populations so that they can make the most appropriate and creative use of Internet tools.

At the policy level, the success of Internet projects in development requires dialogue with national telecommunication agencies to help transform and liberalize the monopolistic telecommunication service environments common in developing countries. Monopolistic services tend to stifle the technological innovation, infrastructure investment and price improvements that often come with competition. Many analysts indicate that where telecommunication reforms have occurred, telecommunication services have "expanded and improved at a faster pace, productivity has increased, new services have become available, and in some cases, international capital markets have been tapped effectively.

A communication for development methodology typically begins with partnerships with local people and organizations to assist them in developing local communication processes by using tools such as community radio and small format video. At the same time, these initiatives work in concert with projects to create national agricultural information and communication networks that strengthen information sharing both horizontally and vertically. Such integrated approaches are achieving important economic and social benefits for rural users, while enabling national agencies to realize significant interorganizational efficiencies.

Communication for development methodologies deserve wider understanding. They are linked to participatory development methodologies and resemble basic computer systems analysis approaches which should start with the needs of computer users. Communication for development methodologies do, however, provide development planners with a conceptual approach that puts rural people, rural organizations farmers and agricultural organizations in positions where they can help direct communication and information network development. Communication for development methodologies can be important factors in achieving sustainable development:

An integrated rural Internet development approach also requires leadership among individuals who can put aside considerations of institutional competition. Such leaders must demonstrate, through action, their belief in the value of information sharing over information hoarding, and their dedication to rural and agricultural development. Without enthusiastic champions, most Internet projects will fail. It is not enough for development planners to build wonderful network systems and provide people with computers and modems. Potential users must identify with a vision for beneficial applications, and they are most likely to respond to the visions of enthusiastic peers and colleagues. This vast project was initially led by only three young civil servants with a small budget and the support of a handful of high level government champions. In its early stages the project met with a great deal of resistance across many ministries. Despite resistance, the project staff worked diligently to identify and empower institutional champions, most of whom were located at relatively low levels within the Government.

Within two years, almost every Government ministry had at least one champion working to place useful information on the Internet and strengthen links between ministries and with the public. As the public became more adept at accessing available Government information, they began to demand more resources, while often providing vocal praise for the initiatives underway. Before long, a momentum had developed that could no longer be resisted by reluctant bureaucrats, and eventually the provision of government information on the Internet became a matter of public policy. Parallel federal and provincial government efforts to strengthen community, private sector and educational access to the Internet helped push further demands for government information, along with mechanisms for engaging the government in new forms of electronic dialogue.

Rural communities around the world tend to be under serviced in their access to the various technologies, Internet services and telecommunication connections that help transmit those services. In Canada, poor Internet access relates directly to a poor rural telecommunication infrastructure. This situation is the result of antiquated telephone lines in many rural areas combined with a general policy myopia about the needs and desires of rural people. Several developing countries have better rural telecommunication systems than many parts of rural Canada.

This situation is changing quickly, and the Internet is the catalyst. Rural peoples' desires to use the Internet are resulting in unprecedented and vocal demands for rural telecommunication improvements. In Canada, strong rural Internet champions are emerging from agricultural producer organizations rural economic development agencies, health care groups and educational bodies. Their advocacy efforts are quickly leading to change and to government and private sector support for rural telecommunication enhancement and Internet support services. In the last eighteen months, over 50 rural and agricultural producer organizations in the province of Ontario alone have joined the Internet community by establishing electronic information resources.

The Internet has sparked an unprecedented interest in telecommunication infrastructure among people who previously had little interest in telephone wires. A decade ago telephone systems could only be expected to carry voice conversations between two people. Now they are expected to move vast libraries of information, photographs, music and even video while enabling dozens of people to communicate with one another at the same time. Where once we could tolerate static and interference during a telephone call over poor rural telephone lines, we tend to become quickly frustrated by the very same lines when they are responsible for limiting our access to information and multiple communication channels.

The demand for telecommunication improvement tends to be most acute among those who are most marginalized from information resources and communication services: rural people, rural organizations and farmers' groups. People who once had very little interest in telecommunication infrastructure are now learning what they need to know to advocate for the communication and information tools they desire. In some cases, rural people and farmers take it upon themselves to create their "homegrown" services when established telecommunication bodies do not meet the demand. Evidence of this can be found throughout the developing world. Examples include the entrepreneurial farmers in Zambia who are working to create a rural telecommunication infrastructure based on new digital wireless and fiber optic technologies, and farmers in northern Mexico who have created an Internet service to enable producer organizations to better communicate and access market information.

Development Initiatives

Investments in development require vision. Development initiatives that involve technology will sometimes lose sight of the human dimensions of development. The goal of an integrated approach to improving Internet services for rural and agricultural development is to enable rural people to increase the community resources they require to improve their lives. Communication networks that enable information to flow to and from rural communities and agricultural organizations as well as between and among the many intermediary organizations that touch rural communities and farmers directly or indirectly, will strengthen community resources. This requires a vision of all the stakeholders involved in rural and agricultural development communicating with one another, with rural organizations and people having access to the same communication tools and information resources as their urban peers.

The Internet suits this vision well. The Internet is a medium of communication, and is perhaps the most flexible medium currently available. It has the potential for integration within a wide variety of projects that have objectives such as local participation, training, education, research (especially participatory research), technical support and institutional strengthening. In short, it is a tool that can be of value to integrated rural and agricultural development. Whenever a project involves people who need to communicate and share information across geography, across social groupings, between organizations and throughout production systems, there is a need to create flexible systems of communication and information sharing. Thus, projects that might find a role for Internet applications could range from apiculture training to community forestry to veterinary medicine.

The Internet is a multipurpose tool that, in its essence, enables people to learn from one another and work together. The results of Internet projects are not technical, but human and social. The Internet is essentially a tool for enhancing human relationships. Projects need to be driven, not by technical concerns, but by human knowledge, communication, and social relationship concerns. Thus, the intended results of an Internet project ought to relate directly to improvements in social relationships, improvements in knowledge sharing and knowledge access, and enhancement of communication among people and organizations. Such project results can happen through efforts to increase rural community resources and agricultural resources to achieve project outputs (depending upon local circumstances) such as:

— locally developed learning tools, learning games, learning networks;

— interactive and collaborative extension information networks among farmer organizations government extension services, rural media, research bodies and educational institutions;

— rural "folk schools" and "farmer field schools" similar to those created by rural radio, and non-formal education initiatives such as farm radio forums and radio listening groups;

— market information networks (regional, national, local);

— distance learning programmes and networks;

— participatory research and action networks;

— interactive and collaborative "expert systems" and decision-support networks;

— early warning system information dissemination and data gathering networks;

— shared curriculum databases and curriculum development networks; research sharing and information dissemination systems;

— training tools;

— small and medium enterprise development networks and marketing mechanisms;

— rural media networks (e.g. rural radio, newsletters, etc.);

— agro-ecosystem health networks;

— indigenous knowledge networks;

— disease and pest monitoring action networks (plant and animal); water management information networks;

— agricultural product and service trading networks (regional, national, local).

Improving rural community information and communication resources must also link to efforts to improve the capacity of rural organizations and rural people to make the most effective, and sustainable, use of those resources. Internet initiatives for rural and agricultural development need to be approached with a degree of caution. Different regions, organizations and communities will have different application, capacity building and technical needs. In some areas it is possible to have farmers and rural residents as direct Internet users (e.g. Chile, Mexico). In other areas, the challenge will be to help build the capacity of intermediary organizations (such as extension field offices, NGOs, rural schools, libraries, health clinics, government satellite offices, and church organizations or assist in the establishment and promotion of community information centres linked to the Internet. In all cases, it will be important to link Internet activities with existing media and local communication methods and patterns.

Every initiative is likely to have its own unique characteristics as a result of the unique characteristics of the local people involved and their social, cultural and economic backgrounds. Special attention also needs to be given to women's involvement in these initiatives. Overall, there are more male Internet users than female Internet users. North American surveys place the ratio in that region of the world at between three and four to one, male to female Internet users. This situation seems to be improving over time. However, special efforts must be made to insure that women have a chance for early participation in new Internet initiatives for rural and agricultural development. Concern for gender equity is one reason for this recommendation. Another is evidence which suggests that women can play a role in ensuring that community oriented Internet services remain focused on community needs and do not get carried away by technological gimmickry.

FAO's twenty-five year experience with a communication for development approach to rural and agricultural communication, using media such as rural radio, small format video (participatory video), photography and print, is now being applied to the Internet in three small scale initiatives. This simple and common-sense strategy of involving people in assessments of their knowledge and communication needs is the cornerstone of communication for development methodologies. Much of FAO's success with communication for development approaches has involved the use of a medium that many development planners first dismissed as too "high-tech" and as being inappropriate technology. This medium is small format video (consumer grade video cameras and portable television monitors). Facilitators use small format video to enable rural residents to articulate their ideas, aspirations, needs and solutions.

Using video, people can speak directly to distant decision makers and researchers, gain access to knowledge presented in audiovisual form by experts (often other farmers), and share their experiences with one another across distances. In participatory video work, the communication process is more important than the production of a video. This aspect of the process is frequently misunderstood by observers of communication for development projects. It is not important for participants to become communication professionals: the goal is to provide media that are flexible enough to allow people to articulate and share their ideas.

Integrated into development planning activities, such a communication for development approach enables farmers and rural people to actively participate in development processes. These approaches enable rural stakeholders to articulate their knowledge, organize local activities, take part in decision making and fully recognize the value of sharing their ideas. Like participatory video processes, the Internet may help people to attain their development goals, but it must be used as a communication process tool and not simply as a static "information technology." Otherwise, Internet tools will be relegated to the junk heaps of inappropriate development technologies or dismissed because of previous failures to make the medium locally relevant and useful.

If, for example, the information outputs derived from highly technical electronic information systems such as famine early warning systems or food security databases are not made available to the people whose lives are the subject of those systems, then we are failing to fully exploit the large infrastructure investments involved, and we are failing to assist people in making appropriate decisions based on such valuable information. Before we even create such tools, we ought to involve the ultimate beneficiaries in determining the value of these initiatives and discussing planning approaches.

A fact that is well known to current Internet users is that the Internet has the power to cut across social and geographic distance and help people find new ways of facilitating the flow of information and knowledge. In many ways the Internet has always been a development communication tool. Within bureaucratic organizations it has a way of levering hierarchies, facilitating new communication patterns, and helping enable activities that might not otherwise occur. This factor makes it an especially attractive medium within communication for development efforts. The key to achieving similar results in new Internet and development projects is to begin with a grassroots, beneficiary-inclusive communication for development approach during the planning process.

Internet and Development Initiatives

The range of locally initiated Internet services in developing countries is remarkable. Many of these services have emerged with little or no external support, and many have become viable commercial services or not-for-profit services operated by NGOs. A large number of these Internet services have been around for almost a decade, coming into existence years before most donor agencies recognized any potential in the Internet as a development tool. Today, however, many international development agencies and international NGOs are finding ways to assist in the development and strengthening of local Internet services, infrastructure and information providers.

Despite the wide range of organizations supporting Internet services and applications in developing countries, obtaining accurate and up-to-date information on these activities is difficult. Donor agencies and project staff are not communicating about their initiatives very well. Despite the obvious potential of the Internet for sharing information on Internet projects, there is no single source that enables interested parties to quickly access information on specific projects, country activities and donor agency strategies and plans. As a result, the lessons being learned are being lost. Leaders in the donor agency community must remedy this problem soon to ensure that lessons learned are shared and that interested parties can quickly and easily identify opportunities for collaboration and for using Internet services and applications in developing countries.

The Internet was conceived in 1963 by Larry Roberts while he was working for the Advanced Research Projects Agency (ARPA) with funding from the United States Department of Defence. The fact that, at its essence, the Internet is a human relationship enhancement tool is reflected in its history, and the very human relationships of its early developers. ARPAnet, as it was called in the beginning, emerged as a communication tool in the late 1960s for a handful of Defence workers and contractors. It was designed as a fundamentally *decentralized* network in order to be a fail-safe communication system.

Computers could send packets of information from one computer to another, across the United States, and those packets could travel through a variety of different routes to reach their destination. If one or several routes were destroyed or malfunctioning, the packets would find alternative routes and eventually reach their destinations. The wife of one of the ARPAnet engineers was hearing impaired. To communicate with her while he was at the office and she was at home, the engineer used a telephone attachment that was then commonly used in the United States. A telephone text messaging device (TTY) enabled him and his wife to converse through text messages sent through the telephone system. This relationship enhancing tool influenced the engineer to incorporate text messaging between people (not just between computers) as a feature of ARPAnet. This feature became known as electronic mail or e-mail, and now millions of e-mail messages cries-cross the globe every day. As a result of one person's positive experience with a similar relationship enhancing tool, what was initially a tool for computers to talk to computers became a tool for enhancing relationships.

ARPAnet grew during the late 1960s and throughout the 1970s because new "nodes" and routes were added to reach university researchers. As a wider community of faculty members and students outside the Department of Defence began to use the tool, electronic mail quickly gained popularity across university and college campuses in North America. Because it was a decentralized network, there was little way to control its popular expansion, and it soon transcended its Department of Defence mentors. The Internet today is a peoples' network. Anyone with basic computer equipment and a phone line can connect to it, communicate through it, host information on it, and look through it.

Unlike many other media, such as television and radio, every user of the medium can be an information producer and knowledge sharer. No one knows for sure how many people are using the Internet today, but estimates range from 50 to 100 million people, and it is growing fast. In countries such as Thailand, Internet use is growing at a current rate of close to 1 000 percent per year. The Internet is essentially millions of people connected together via millions of computers that are connected together.

There are at least five million information-containing computers serving information to the millions and millions of Internet users. Each of those five million computers may contain thousands, or hundreds of thousands of pages of information. If current trends continue, there will be over 100 million computers connected to the Internet by the year 2000. Any one of those computers linked to the Internet might support one individual or thousands of individuals, together with the wealth of information they can contribute to the Internet. There are two powerful tools that form the basis of the Internet. The earliest on the scene, and still the most popular, is e-mail. Using a simple address to guide them, e-mail messages jump from computer to computer, rapidly finding their way to their recipients.

The more recent tool, and the one that has catapulted the Internet into popular culture, is the World Wide Web. The World Wide Web is the part of the Internet where we are witnessing the emergence of a vast global library of information. Electronic publishing of information on the World Wide Web is much less expensive than print publication. It is also very easy to become a provider of information on the World Wide Web and have people use your information almost instantaneously from virtually any location in the world. As a result, the World Wide Web is propagated with information on every subject imaginable.

In fact, an Internet user who wants to publish a work can do so for little or no money and make that work available around the globe. The World Wide Web is in its infancy, having only been developed in 1994, yet only three years after its birth it is one of the most popular information sharing tools in the world. Use of the World Wide Web is growing at a rate of 25 percent per month and it is estimated that some 100 to 400 new information sites are established on the World Wide Web each week. Prior to the World Wide Web, Internet users were limited to e-mail communication and cumbersome methods for retrieving files of information from other computers.

The World Wide Web changed that quite dramatically. Now we can retrieve information, documents, and a wide variety of audiovisual material simply by pointing and clicking. We do not even have to know the location of the computer from which we retrieve information. We just click on a highlighted word, or a picture, and within moments a document is transported to the screen in front of us. Some argue that the Internet's World Wide Web is humanity's second major communication revolution, the first being the Gutenburg Press in 1439.

Compared to the costs of using telephones or faxes, communicating and sharing information using e-mail or the World Wide Web can be hundreds of times less expensive. Because information flows through the Internet in discrete packets of digital bits, those packets are able to share telecommunication lines with hundreds of other packets. Where a traditional transatlantic telephone call will tie up a single phone line for only two people, an e-mail message can travel along a phone line with hundreds and even thousands of other messages. Some creative computer software developers have even made use of this feature of the Internet to create Internet telephone services that allow users to speak with other users around the globe, while completely avoiding long distance phone charges.

Elements of Successful Rural and Agricultural Internet Communication

Twelve common elements can be identified among successful rural and agricultural Internet communication and information svstems:

1. Preliminary participatory communication and information needs assessments with intended users.
2. Awareness building campaigns designed to sensitize decision makers to the possible uses of Internet services.
3. Executing agency commitment to participatory rural and agricultural development.
4. Local "champions" identified and supported.
5. Open participation of user community in design, implementation and management of communication and information services.
6. Institutional and user commitment to manage and sustain Internet services.
7. Involvement of the full community of users, including women and youth.
8. Ongoing provision for technical training, user support and outreach within the user community.
9. Combination of centralized and decentralized information production, analysis and distribution.
10. Ongoing provision for technical support and system maintenance/ upgrading.
11. User community financial commitment in communication and information systems (e.g. ownership of hardware, user fees, salaries, infrastructure, etc.).
12. Social service orientation of local private sector or not-for-profit (university or NGO) Internet service providers.

Local private sector or not-for-profit Internet service providers tend to be able to operate efficiently and profitably while providing customers with reasonable service prices. They are able to quickly troubleshoot and solve service problems, they can access capital through investment and credit (not as easily obtained with government-focused or donor agency services), and they are able to offer strong local user support, customer troubleshooting (often with house calls), and local training. Because they are dependent upon customer revenue for profitability, they are likely to respond quickly to customer needs and demands. Government operated ISPs tend to be less able to meet customer needs and are often less responsive because they have other sources of support than customer fees. Local private sector and not-for-profit ISPs also contribute to the local economy and stimulate local interest in telecommunication through personal contacts and relationships.

In 1994, as part of FAO's Latin American communication for development effort, community animators initiated an extensive participatory communication and information needs assessment among six hundred local farmers and their organizations The results indicated that farmers strongly desired an improved communication system, and local leaders required a better management communication system for organizing activities and for agricultural and irrigation planning among 23 local organizations The farmers also wanted better methods for general communication and information sharing to assist in the planning of current and future work and activities. One strategy that they proposed was a computer-based communication system that would provide for both horizontal and vertical communication.

A communication for development expert from FAO provided initial logistical coordination and technical backstopping for the first nine months of the initiative. A computer network server was installed at the university and each farmer organization was issued an account for dial-in access to a small pool of three modems connected to the server. By June of 1996, 12 farmers' organizations were connected and using the system, several World Wide Web information services were available, and plans were being made to improve the system and involve all 23 farmers' organizations in the Rio Colorado Valley. Existing users make use of e-mail on a daily basis, and submit daily reports on irrigation quotas and planting activities to the local irrigation water authority.

The farmers are proud of their community and its history, so they decided to organize a photography contest to collect historical photographs of the region and its agricultural heritage to place on their World Wide Web homepage. They are planning to post their newsletters on the homepage as well, and hope to provide easy access to locally relevant market and weather information. Links will soon be made with the Technical Information and Communication Unit (TICU) to expand access to TICU's market information bulletin (currently distributed in Sonora by fax) by placing bulletin information on the CETYS University server for access throughout Mexico and the world (personal communication with Emilio Canton, FAO-Mexico).

These farmers' organizations have proven that Internet communication and information services are practical and beneficial when developed with full participation of users. While the system has a long way to go in order to develop further applications and enhance user involvement with new applications, it is already attracting significant interest within the Mexican Ministry of Agriculture and other farmer organizations in Mexico. For example, Assistance and Services for Agricultural Marketing (ASERCA) is investigating the Mexicali experience in order to develop strategies for expanding farmer access to electronic information services related to marketing and the development of national and international trading links.

There are even plans for developing an electronic trading system for agricultural products and services. The development communication approach used to form the

Mexicali system is the key to its initial success and its future sustainability. Using this approach has enabled the organizational leaders to fully understand the value of the system and its applications, and led to the farmers' decision to take ownership of the infrastructure and network development.

These networks provide farmer organizations with data on crops, international crop status and market timing, prices, market conditions (regional, national, international), weather, technical and training information, and information about the various organizations that support their work. The users also have full access to the Internet to find other information relevant to their lives and communities (e.g. health, social service, education, etc.), and they can use electronic mail to communicate with other farm organizations in Chile, as well as any of the millions of people using the global Internet.

The most important aspect of this initiative is its specific attention to local information needs assessments, and provision of assistance to farm organization personnel to help them develop the skills necessary to analyse and disseminate information that is locally relevant. This methodology emerged from previous development communication experiences using small format video, print media and rural radio. It is very likely the most user oriented approach to developing Internet services in the developing world, and it is focused on rural and remote agricultural communities that would normally have little opportunity to access the benefits of Internet tools.

Small information centres are located within the offices of farmer organizations and NGOs, and some of these offices are beginning to open up their Internet resources to non-agricultural community members such as youth groups and social service agencies. The network of users is currently small (five organizations and may become a model for the development of a much wider network within

Chile, and, with some external assistance, throughout Latin America. Much of the information available through the Chilean network is useful to other Spanish speaking Internet users (the same is true for the Mexican initiatives discussed above).

The Mexican and Chilean experiences are unique examples of using a communication for development approach to create horizontal and vertical communication systems for small producers and rural and remote communities. Throughout the other countries visited on the author's FAO fact-finding mission, it was generally observed that access to the Internet in rural and remote areas is emerging slowly. To their credit, many organizations in Africa, including FAO and its supported projects, are developing World Wide Web based information tools that may someday be of direct benefit to small producers and rural and remote communities.

In Zambia and Zimbabwe, for example, FAO projects are busy developing Internet-based market information tools, household food security information systems, famine early warning systems and ether sophisticated tools to assist decision makers. These systems are developed primarily by researchers and policy making bodies to fulfill their own internal information needs. Thus far, links to the ultimate beneficiaries of these initiatives are weak.

In Africa, local and regional Internet service providers such as ZamNet (which also services the HealthNet project that connects rural health centres to the Internet), SangoNet, MangoNet, Enda-Dakar and Internet Africa, appear to be the only organizations with the tangible experience of providing Internet services to organizations and individuals in rural and remote areas. Their track records speak for themselves. They have managed to provide Internet services to many of the intermediary organizations that serve small producers, rural communities and agricultural organizations.

Many of the field officers of UN agencies and multilateral donor projects make use of electronic mail and Internet information services provided by these local services. The individuals who work within these Internet service providers tend to be extremely dedicated to their work and to improving Internet service in Africa. These services are "natural" examples of the horizontal and vertical communication channels essential to the integrated approach.

Future Internet development activities for rural communities and farm organizations in Africa and Latin America ought to begin with the experiences and services of existing Internet service providers and existing user groups. There is a wealth of experience, talent, creativity and local understanding available, and development agencies would be wise to utilize these resources at every opportunity.

Internet Applications for Sustainable Development

With regard to Internet use in support of rural and agricultural development, applications fall into five main areas: economic development for agricultural producers, community development, research/education, small and medium enterprise (SME) development, and media networks. Rural communities and small-scale agricultural producers are deeply affected by global economic, environmental and political forces. The idea that communities of small-scale agricultural producers are isolated and living in closed, self-sufficient societies is a myth. Global trade relationships, such as GATT, NAFTA, and MERCOSUR, place rural communities and small-scale agricultural producers squarely in the middle of global market realities. Trade decisions in Rome or Chicago today affect campesinos in Mexico within hours. Interest rates, global commodity situations, changing trade patterns, transportation developments and tariff structures all impact upon even the smallest farm operation. Without knowledge and without the communication capabilities required to access, analyse and share the information required to create knowledge, small producers remain at the mercy of global market forces.

With knowledge, small producers can have a competitive footing with larger farm operations and corporate agriculture. Small producers often have the flexibility to quickly change crop choices, develop products for small niche markets and even market directly to the consumer or commodity broker in distant countries. Small-scale, labour intensive farming can reduce input costs and provide consumers with higher food quality, improved food safety and better food taste. When knowledge is harnessed by strong organizations of small producers, strategic planning can be used to provide members with lower cost inputs, better storage facilities, improved transportation links and collective negotiations with buyers. Organizations of small producers want and need instant information on global market prices, negotiation techniques and strategies, analyses of product potentials in various markets, new production and marketing techniques, new transportation systems, and global trade rules.

Information that can reduce the costs of transactions and improve prices received at markets (or open new markets) is highly valued. These organizations can and do act as communication conduits or intermediaries, facilitating the flow of information between local people and the rest of the world. The global Internet is one tool that can enhance this flow of information for organizations of small producers. It is an inexpensive way to communicate and access global information. Local Internet services can be easily managed by well-organized local user groups and farmer organizations. Information and analyses can be tailored to local, regional and national knowledge and communication needs and realities. When combined with national and global market information systems, and with the ability to communicate quickly with potential buyers and brokers, local Internet systems become valuable strategic planning and decision making tools.

Local agricultural producers can benefit from the Internet without having access to computers or phone lines. Community information centre personnel can easily post market prices at places where farmers gather, can liaise with local radio stations and newspapers, and can channel information through interpersonal networks, simple newsletters and posters. Used wisely, the Internet can be part of an extended media mix for both gathering information from vertical channels and disseminating information through existing horizontal communication channels.

Applications of Community Development

Local community oriented Internet services are also valuable when placed in the service of rural and agricultural development organizations which act as local communication conduits or intermediaries. Along with providing improved market knowledge, they can also:

— develop locally appropriate applications and creative services;

— provide knowledge about successful development strategies;

— enable efficient regional, national and global organizational efforts (the use of the Internet as a global communication and organising tool in Chiapas, Mexico is an excellent example of the latter);

— provide improved access to a huge variety of information, training, research and educational resources (including distance education services) that are typically unavailable in rural and remote areas due to the costs associated with accessing printed materials and books;

— enable rural young people to learn about computers and to have access to the technologies and information available to their urban peers;

— provide access to critical technical information for rural professionals such as physicians, health care workers, technicians and engineers, thereby providing further encouragement for these professionals to continue practicing in rural and remote communities;

— be used as marketing tools to promote rural tourism and market the products of small secondary industries and home-based businesses;

— enable local NGOs to gain a global presence and make better contact with potential donors and supporters through on-line publication of resources and information, and through the use of electronic mail; and

— sensitize urban policy makers to the realities and needs of rural populations.

Within national, regional and international research communities, there is increased attention toward "participatory research" strategies. These strategies place farmers and rural residents at the centre of the research process and enable them to enrich their knowledge base and share that knowledge with one another, field workers, researchers and decision-makers at various levels. Internet use among intermediary organizations and leaders involved in participatory research can provide a cost effective method for documenting and sharing lessons learned and research results. Internet use also has the potential to strengthen linkages between and among farmer organizations extension workers, researchers, policy makers and other actors in a farming system. For example, international organizations such as the Information Centre for Low-

External-Input and Sustainable Agriculture (ILEIA).

The cost of accessing printed academic materials within developing countries is usually so high that students and faculty members have great difficulty acquiring books and journals. Also, the time required to obtain printed materials from overseas can be long enough to render some information out-dated by the time it arrives. Via the Internet, information published on-line can be accessed almost instantly and at a small fraction of the cost of obtaining printed materials. Information on the Internet is easy to access and archival lists of resources can be easily reviewed and assessed in remote locations.

Electronic distance education services are already in use in North America, Australia and Europe (particularly among people in rural areas), and with the continued growth of Internet access in developing countries, there is a very good chance that similar services will develop significant demand. Over 87 percent of the rural Internet users involved in the University of Guelph's Rural Internet User Survey indicated that they were very interested in taking advantage of on-line courses and other structured learning opportunities via the Internet, yet there are few such opportunities available to meet their level of interest.

Overall, the Internet holds significant potential to enhance learning and research relationships among researchers, academics and students, wherever they are located. The list of potential applications is infinite and thousands of informal linkages of this sort take place every day on Internet discussion groups. Development agencies can play a role in helping to formalize and provide credentials and diplomas for people who participate in specific electronic learning initiatives delivered via the Internet.

Within FAO's Sustainable Development Department, for example, there are existing training and curriculum development projects focused on communication for development and extension worker training. Other FAO departments and many other agencies have similar projects. The materials and processes created within these projects can be adapted for Internet distance education delivery. Such distance education projects could take advantage of the power of the Internet to facilitate local and international learner interaction and team learning contexts based on group learning projects, as opposed to the traditional correspondence style of distance education.

Enterprise Development

Private sector businesses, large and small, are using the Internet to reach new markets, promote products and services globally, and access critical business and financial information. Rural food producers in North America now use the Internet to sell a wide variety of products including live lobsters and packages of apples, oranges, grapefruit, cheeses, smoked meats, pastries and pies. Producers of rural crafts and manufactured goods sell everything from clothing to furniture over the Internet, and use the Internet to organize support networks. The Internet represents a global storefront for such rural and remote businesses, providing them with a degree of access to customers never before possible.

The tourism sector has been quick to recognize the benefits of the Internet for advertising destinations, tours and holiday services. For all of the countries visited during his recent FAO Internet fact-finding mission, the author was able to make use of World Wide Web travel information from the host countries in order to make travel plans. With full colour pictures, and information on hotels, weather, attractions, events, travel tips, currency conversion rates, visa information and much more, travelers are able to obtain timely and accurate information and make informed destination choices.

Of particular interest are the World Wide Web sites for "ecotourism," game parks, and adventure tours in rural areas of Southern Africa where rural tourism is a growing industry. Tourism operators in rural and remote areas have a difficult time marketing their destinations through traditional media due to production and distribution costs. The Internet now represents a very inexpensive way for them to showcase their sites to the world and interact directly with potential tourists.

The news media in developing countries have also been on the forefront of developing Internet applications. Internet service providers (IPS) use the Internet to source news stories from local writers in developing countries and share those stories with international wire services such as Associated Press. IPS is also able to provide Internet feeds that enable African news media to have access to African news from around the continent. This is particularly relevant to rural radio stations and other rural newspaper and newsletter producers that would otherwise have been unable to obtain the same news from other sources. IPS can also provide an outlet for rural news writers to share their stories regionally, nationally and globally. Similar Internet strategies for rural radio networks, which might also incorporate digital audio transmissions, may well emerge in the near future.

Development of Internet Initiatives

At the end of the Twentieth Century, people in rural and remote areas of developing countries are facing many unprecedented challenges brought on by the changing global economy, dynamic political contexts, environmental degradation and demographic pressures. The number of food insecure around the world continues to increase. To deal with these challenges, and to make critical decisions, people at all levels of society, and especially the food insecure and the organizations that serve and represent them, must be able to access critical information and communicate. Improved communication and information access are directly related to social and economic development. Participatory development is fully dependent upon communication and information sharing processes.

One cannot expect poor farmers and food insecure residents of rural communities to list computers and digital telecommunication services as high priority items for improving their lives. However, there exist various intermediaries that serve these populations which, together with small and medium enterprises (SMEs) in rural areas, can take advantage of these technologies to improve their work, improve communication capacity, gain efficiencies and reduce telecommunication costs. An integrated approach that fosters horizontal and vertical channels of communication is key to insuring that such benefits are realized.

Intermediary organizations such as extension field offices, rural NGOs, health clinics, government offices, and church organizations together with SMEs, can offer benefit to their rural client groups in numerous ways. Strategies for improving Internet access and use for rural and agricultural development will necessarily involve full participation of intermediary organizations and other rural stakeholders. As Internet services become more widely used among these organizations it becomes more important to facilitate the exchange of lessons learned and best practices that emerge from on-the-ground experience.

The following are the 11 activities to assist rural stakeholders in gaining access to, and developing creative uses for, Internet services:

— Promote regional coordination of Internet strategy for rural and agricultural development.

— Establish pilot projects.

— Use a communication for development approach.

— Support efforts to liberalize telecommunication policies in developing countries.

— Support local Internet entrepreneurs and other service providers in developing countries.

— Assist stakeholders in advocating for Internet service provision and telecommunication infrastructure and policy improvements.

— Orient existing Internet information services to users in developing countries.

— Support rural and agricultural education sector Internet capability.

— Provide Internet awareness building and demonstration.

— Support rural and remote infrastructure development.

— Support creative Internet applications and information services for rural and agricultural development.

Policy and Regional Coordination of Internet Strategy for Rural and Agricultural Development

The Internet expansion in the developing world is led primarily by non-governmental organizations universities, and private sector Internet service providers (ISPs). These organizations are typically small and underfunded, but manage to utilize new and emerging technologies to provide reliable Internet services to civil society at competitive rates. With little or no donor support they have emerged as the most effective and sustainable service providers in developing countries.

Governments participate, directly or indirectly, through the provision of improved telecommunication services (such as fibre optic and satellite backbones), improved policy and regulatory environments that enable private sector initiatives, information and communication technology consulting centres, information and communication technology assistance to the educational sector, and in some cases government telecom Internet service (such as Senegal). Rural and remote regions, however, experience many barriers to receiving the benefits of Internet services. For example, many African capital cities have reasonably reliable Internet services available, but outside such centralized focal points, service is poor or nonexistent.

Donor agencies can play important roles in influencing national policy with regard to rural and agricultural development and national telecommunication improvement strategies. For example, they can:

— encourage governments to support private sector knowledge and communication technology innovations and services targeted to rural and agricultural communities;

— encourage the creation of national information and technology consulting centres, and work to ensure that such centres target some of their services to under served communities;

— encourage national agricultural research centres (NARS) to investigate the potential of national research knowledge systems and participatory research systems via the Internet;

— encourage governments involved in telecommunication service improvement to recognise the needs of rural and agricultural communities for service upgrades;

— encourage governments to involve women and women's organizations in the development of Internet and telecommunication strategy development and activities;

— assist national educational sectors in establishing rural and agricultural knowledge and information systems learning programmes in universities and technical schools, as well as assist in developing innovative rural learning programme delivery strategies such as electronic distance education;

— encourage governments to utilize knowledge and communication technology for administrative improvement, extension, and for civil society liaison within rural and agricultural communities (via existing field, extension, research and administrative offices).

Recently, many funding and aid agencies have been "jumping on the Internet bandwagon" to support a collage of Internet related projects in Africa and Latin America. Only recently have some of these agencies begun supporting coordinated and collaborative activities to support establishment and enhancement of Internet services to rural and remote areas (e.g. IDRC in partnership with FAO in Southern Africa). These areas are, however, the locations with the greatest need for improved communication and information services. Assisting in the coordinated establishment and enhancement of Internet services to rural and remote areas is an activity that donors can support to achieve many benefits for rural populations. In doing so, donor agencies can ensure that their initiatives take advantage of the gains made by other agencies, while serving a sector - the people of rural areas - that may otherwise continue to be neglected.

International Development Research Centre (IDRC) contains a number of useful recommendations for regional coordination of strategy in Africa, including:

— achieve commitment among development agencies to collaborate on a clear strategy for information and communication technology support in Africa in order to improve planning and resource sharing and eliminate the current "overlap in the multiplicity of projects in certain countries and activities";

— improve the availability of information on the existing information and communication technology infrastructure and projects;

— improve access to technical skills;

— improve information and communication technology for African use, which can include non-African knowledge network administrators becoming familiar with the specific challenges faced by African or Latin American Internet users to insure that information available in Europe or North America is equally accessible (in terms of speed and consistency) in developing countries;

— increase support for the development of "local content" and the conversion of existing stand-alone computerised information systems to networked access, integration with decision support systems, and development of new information-based services that exploit local potential; and

— develop and publicise key pilot projects.

Internet pilot projects can enable the development of local applications related to the range of outputs suggested above. These projects should start on a small scale (even small investments of US$18 000 are known to achieve important results) which would allow them to be implemented soon, and take advantage of collaborative opportunities with other agencies. Results should be well documented and shared locally, nationally and internationally via reports, videos, Internet World Wide Web sites, and local and international media. Ties to existing Internet services and projects (urban or rural) that involve significant local participation would improve chances of success. Pilot projects should endeavour to involve women and young people (often the most energetic proponents of Internet communication initiatives) in the planning, development and implementation of activities. Small pilot projects will help establish "best practices," provide avenues for sharing "lessons learned," and act as vehicles for expanding the impact of Internet initiatives and enhancing coordination.

Pilot projects can also document and highlight the challenges of supporting participatory communication for development initiatives. Research on impact not only focuses on users and local applications, but also on people who do not participate directly in local Internet initiatives (perhaps older people or people marginalized from power structures) and suggest mechanisms for enabling them to benefit directly or indirectly from these initiatives. Research can also help provide reliable data on the most appropriate technologies and the essential infrastructure requirements for rural Internet services.

The most effective and beneficial Internet communication and information services are managed and operated by the members of the organizations served. User management ensures that information is appropriate, and actually desired, by local users. Many of the information services currently designed to serve rural and agricultural users are created with little or no collaboration with the intended users.

Non-governmental organizations such as farmer associations and cooperatives, that serve rural and agricultural communities, are best suited for developing and providing information and communication services to those communities. Developing information services with users and catalyzing sustainable user management of communication networks is not a common strategy among funding agencies. It is common to find that intended users are unaware of the information and communication services being developed for them. The FAO communication for development approach helps to develop communication and information services that begin with user information needs assessments, and helps to create system ownership and management strategies that are financially sustainable. Mechanisms for providing training and continuous support, delivered for and by the organizations and users involved, are an important part of this approach. It is relatively easy to install the technology for electronic information and communication networks. It is much more difficult to create systems that people actually use and from which they receive tangible benefits.

Connecting small producers and rural residents directly to Internet systems is, for most residents of communities in the developing world, impractical. However, many of the intermediaries (the non-governmental organizations and government units) that serve these people can use Internet systems to provide better services to the people they serve. Organizations that are predisposed to open collaboration with the people they serve can become focal points for information analysis and Internet communication access. Such organizations can become Community Access Telecommunication Services (CATS), providing locally relevant information analysis and dissemination, together with public access to Internet telecommunication services such as electronic mail.

The latter function is emerging as a service in its own right in many developing countries. The "telecentres" of Senegal and the "cybercafes" (simple electronic mail services and World Wide Web access services resembling old telegraph services) of Mexico and Zimbabwe, developed by local entrepreneurs, are examples of such basic telecommunication services. Basic electronic mail services are beginning to replace fax and telegraph services as an extremely low cost medium for sending messages between individuals and organizations As the Internet expands, various forms of CATS, telecentres and cybercafes will find their niche in developing countries where the purchase of a personal computer is beyond the means of most individuals.

The concept of "community information centres" is not new, but the Internet opens new possibilities for establishing such centres in rural areas. A computer, modem and phone line can place an ever-expanding global library of information at the fingertips of people in rural and remote communities where books are seldom seen. People can gain access to the information resources and tools they need to solve their own problems, set their own development agendas and empower themselves through knowledge. Community centres, schools, rural libraries, local NGOs, producer associations, municipal organizations church centres and health clinics can act as local hosts for community information centres.

CAP offers a relatively low-cost method for introducing Internet tools to rural areas. Community organizations submit proposals consisting of action plans, resource needs, evidence of community support and evidence of matching in-kind and cash contributions. Proposals are evaluated on the basis of community needs and evidence of commitment to local projects. Funding is offered to a maximum of US$25 000, with most proposals receiving between US$4 000 to 18 000. CAP encourages communities to partner with universities, schools, libraries, health care institutions and local non-governmental organizations. People in CAP recipient communities are generally enthusiastic about the project and the benefits it brings. Several communities that established simple Internet services in rural resource centres have been successful in catalysing local entrepreneurs to establish community-wide commercial Internet services.

CAP is a community driven funding mechanism. Projects are designed by community members who must determine technical requirements, appropriate community applications and Internet access locations, together with long term financial sustainability frameworks. Rural communities that demonstrate need and have researched their proposals well are most likely to obtain funding. The CAP administrators provide a great deal of support in the way of information about successful CAP project applications, and the facilitation of horizontal channels of communication between CAP communities. Technical support is the responsibility of the community which must identify the most appropriate level and source of technical support. CAP works well because it is a non-paternalistic, community initiated funding model with few bureaucratic layers between the funder and the recipient community. There are lessons to be learned here for donor agencies working in developing countries.

Support efforts to liberalise telecommunication policies in developing countries Digital wireless telephony has reached the stage where it is now less expensive to build a new local wireless telephone infrastructure than it is to build a traditional copper wire telephone infrastructure. For many people in developing countries, their first telephone is hand held, portable and wireless. In Zambia, for example, by the end of 1997, an enlightened group of local entrepreneurs (led by wealthy farmers) will likely be providing digital wireless telephone service to rural and remote regions of the country that have never had telephone infrastructure. This new technology provides basic telephone service for less capital cost than a traditional copper wire infrastructure, and also enables the high speed data communication necessary for Internet access. Early planning for involving Zambia's main Internet provider, ZamNet, in this initiative is underway, making the possibility of full Internet access, to even the most remote rural areas of Zambia, a strong probability by the end of 1997.

In other countries, such as South Africa, wireless telephone booths are providing telephone service to rural and remote areas of SouthAtrica, thus providing basic telecommunication service to all residents of the country.

Fibre optic telecommunication "backbones" and new microwave and satellite telephone systems are making their appearance throughout the developing world, drastically reducing telephone service costs and dramatically improving telephone service quality and reliability. Internet services are enhanced, or begin emerging, as a direct result of these telecommunication improvements. In many cases, demand for Internet access is driving the effort to improve telecommunication infrastructure.

There is a strong correlation between such telecommunication improvements in developing countries and national telecommunication policies that help liberalise telecommunication services. The Zambian wireless telephone initiative is possible because of a telecommunication regulatory environment that enables private sector initiatives and competitive service. Relatively restrictive regulatory environments in Zimbabwe, in contrast, have so far prevented the release of portable telephony, despite significant demand. Uganda and Ghana, countries in which Internet use is increasing exponentially, have also adopted liberalized telecommunication policies.

The Egyptian Government's decision to support private sector Internet service provision is resulting in an explosion of Internet services and parallel growth in Internet subscribers. Countries which have poor Internet access also tend to be countries with monopolistic national telecommunication policies and little or no service competition in the telecommunication sector. Donor agencies have an important role in advocating for liberalized telecommunication policies that enable competition and the growth of private sector telecommunication and Internet services. It is also important to ensure that liberalized telecommunication environments balance competition with the needs of under served populations, including rural and remote communities.

Some of the progressive telecommunication policy initiatives in South Africa, which highlight the needs of under served populations and rural areas could prove to be useful models for governments around the world (both in the North and South). Local entrepreneurs, progressive NGOs and university computing departments in urban centres throughout the developing world are becoming Internet service providers (ISPs), providing dial-up telephone access to the sophisticated graphical, sound and video communication environment of the Internet's World Wide Web, together with basic electronic mail services. In Harare, Zimbabwe, there are three locally owned and operated ISPs. For about US$20 per month any individual or organization with a phone line can have full access to such a service, to send as many e-mail messages as they like and to "surf" the World Wide Web for hours from a computer at their home or office.

Small business people operating telecentres and cybercafes in urban parts of the developing world (e.g. Mexico, Egypt, Zimbabwe, Malaysia and Senegal) are bringing the Internet to people who cannot afford computers. For less than 25 US cents an individual can use a telecentre or cybercafe to send an electronic mail message (e-mail) to any e-mail address in the world. A simple way for donor agencies to support these initiatives would be to advocate that their field offices and project officers use local Internet service providers wherever possible. Not only will they gain access to better knowledge and communication services, but they will be able to learn more about the local Internet user community and about local development information created by local communities. Furthermore, while it might be tempting for donor agencies to fund the direct creation of Internet service provision and infrastructure, this may not serve user communities well. Donors funding Internet projects would be wise to direct their funds to user communities who can then determine the best choice for Internet service provision. This will help insure that Internet service providers remain responsive to the needs of their clients, rather than the other way around.

Despite tremendous technological and service advances in every country in the world (developed or developing), rural and remote areas continue to suffer poor telecommunication infrastructure. In rural and northern parts of Canada (one of the technological powerhouses of new telecommunication advances), for instance, thousands of people continue to do without basic telephone service, or are unable to utilize existing infrastructure to operate fax machines. Poor telecommunication infrastructure is recognised as an important factor in leading people in rural areas to choose to migrate to urban areas. Rural economic development officers in Canada, for example, rank improvements in rural telecommunication infrastructure as more important than either improved health services or improved educational services, and cite poor telecommunication infrastructure as a primary factor in the out migration of professionals and the difficulty in attracting skilled professionals to relocate to rural areas. They also believe that improved rural telecommunication infrastructure is the key to economic development.

In rural areas, access to communication and information sharing systems can provide simple, but dramatic benefits. For example, the HealthNet Internet service that operates in Zambia is able to provide rural health care professionals with access to medical databases and rapid medical advice from specialist physicians around the world. Such information can literally make the difference between life and death. In Mexico and Chile, rural farmers are able to obtain timely and accurate commodity prices from Internet and fax services, and use this information to bargain for prices from brokers that are 15 to 20 percent higher than they were previously able to obtain (personal communication from a Mexican farmer). Such price differences, within an agricultural system with increasing input costs, tight profit margins, and global competition, can make the difference between a farmer staying in business or losing the farm.

In North America, the poor availability of Internet services in rural areas has catalyzed an important advocacy effort among rural and agricultural NGOs for general improvements to telecommunication infrastructure and policy. Technical obstacles to Internet service have focused attention on a history of government and corporate blindness to the telecommunication service needs of rural communities. In Canada, advocacy partnerships have emerged that have forged alliances between rural NGOs, women's groups, national and regional health care agencies, municipal governments, agricultural producer associations, universities, consumer groups, aboriginal communities and government bodies responsible for agriculture and rural development. These advocacy efforts are responsible for significant telecommunication service upgrades, policy improvements and federal and provincial programmes that support rural telecommunication and Internet projects.

In developing countries, organizations such as FAO can play important roles in championing emerging rural stakeholder advocacy efforts, and assisting rural stakeholders in gaining voices on national and regional telecommunication/ Internet advisory bodies. Special attention should be paid to the involvement of rural women and women's organizations that serve rural communities. Orient existing Internet information services to users in developing countries

The global Internet now provides access to a plethora of agricultural and rural development information and discussion services. Information resources on low input agriculture, commodity prices, alternative crops, international crop market patterns (seasonality of specific regions, crop successes and failures, etc.), new techniques, integrated pest management, rural development strategies,

FAO reports and research, and countless other topics are freely available to users around the world. In order for all this information to truly be of benefit to small producers and the people of rural and remote areas, it must be easily available to them and/or to the organizations that serve and represent their interests.

One of the common complaints among Internet users within the development communities of developing nations is that the people at the agencies who provide access to this information via the Internet do not know very much about the difficulty of accessing Internet services outside of headquarters or central offices. The speed of information retrieval in Africa is vastly slower than it is within FAO headquarters, for example. While Internet access is expanding rapidly in developing countries, users do not tend to have access to the same range of high speed telecommunication lines and phone lines that are available in the North. Internet "bandwidth" (a function of the size and speed of telecommunication lines) is generally less in developing countries than it is in the North.

Low bandwidth translates into longer transmission times, and for many users in developing countries, increased costs. As one interviewee told the author "in Uganda it costs US$50 an hour to sit in an Internet traffic jam". One remedy for the bandwidth problem, and one that has a relatively minor cost, is to "mirror" information on regionally located servers that could be managed by local Internet service providers. The service providers could gain some much needed revenue, and local users would have dramatically improved retrieval speeds which would encourage use and analysis of the information that is available to them from development agencies.

Many World Wide Web international development and agricultural knowledge resources are exceedingly difficult to access from within developing countries because they are laden with graphics that transfer slowly across the

Internet. This effectively prevents access to the valuable information that lies behind those images. Involving intended Internet information users in developing countries (especially, in the case of FAO, those from rural and agricultural communities) in the design and development of Internet information dissemination techniques is uncommon among development agencies. User consultation methodologies should be developed, and employed as a matter of course, to ensure that users are consulted on an ongoing basis. This will help to avoid user frustration and win user confidence that agency claims to having an understanding of developing country contexts are in fact true.

The most important current Internet user group consists of recent university and college graduates. These individuals are exposed to Internet benefits while at school, and when they obtain jobs in business or government, they encourage the adoption of new technologies and methodologies. Their creative uses of information and communication technology is often adopted by managers and colleagues. Indeed, within any organization one is likely now to find recent graduates leading the way with Internet adoption efforts. Their enthusiasm for the Internet can potentially have far-reaching benefits, and is worthy of development agency support.

In Hermosillo, Mexico for example, three dedicated recent university graduates continue to work full time to provide a valuable agricultural information service despite the fact that they have not received a salary in over eight months. Within FAO's project in Chile, one young woman who recently graduated from a social communication programme, and with no previous computer experience, is primarily responsible for the technical development of information resources currently available to farmer organizations Much of her technical support comes from other young Internet users in other countries with whom she communicates via electronic mail. Throughout the organizations visited during his FAO fact-finding mission, the author consistently found young, recent university graduates playing key roles in the development of local Internet initiatives.

Internet support activities must take account of the availability of dedicated young people, and involve recent graduates wherever possible. Many urban young people, who might not normally be interested in working in rural areas, are excited about the possibility of working with modern communication tools in rural communities. IDRC, for example, is considering developing an international "Internet Youth Corps" to assist in the spread of Internet services in Africa. Activities can also focus on assisting students to gain access to Internet tools.

For the purpose of diffusing Internet services to rural and remote areas, educational institutions in those areas, together with urban educational institutions that have programmes of study related to those areas (e.g. rural development, agriculture, forestry, fisheries, etc.), and research organizations with links to the educational sector (such as national agriculture research centres), could be provided with assistance in acquiring networking computers, training and technical support targeted to young users. Support could also be provided to enable in-course students to engage in practical Internet projects and internships in rural and remote areas. Not only would services be expanded, but local educational institutions would gain a new awareness of rural and agricultural development needs.

In Mexicali, Mexico, for example the university hosting the technical infrastructure for the agricultural communication and information services is now considering offering courses in agricultural communication for development and agricultural marketing. Activities should make a strong effort to involve recent graduates and students in as many ways as possible. Their efforts, creativity, and visions will help ensure success and sustainability.

Despite the rapid growth in Internet service, general awareness of the Internet and its benefits is weak in developing countries. Ties between existing Internet user groups and the rest of the civil society are poor, and there is very little local information content available on the Internet to help stimulate local interest. Existing Internet services have difficulty marketing the Internet beyond early adopters because it often requires fostering desires and needs among clients who may not know they can benefit from the Internet. Thus, awareness building, through workshops, seminars, training courses, public events and media attention, can help to better inform potential user groups and bring them closer to making the decision to begin using the Internet.

Awareness among national non-governmental organizations (NGOs), and rural development and agricultural extension services, is particularly weak. These groups should be specifically targeted for awareness building initiatives, and it is here that agencies such as FAO can play an important role through their existing relationship with such groups. Findings from the author's fact-finding mission and research lead to the premise that the majority of current Internet users in developing countries belong to one of the following groups:

— recent university or college graduates (both nationals and non-nationals);

— internationally funded non-governmental organizations (NGOs); international development projects supported by major donor agencies; international organizations;

— government units with staff and contacts among the above-mentioned groups;

- universities and the educational sector in general; researchers;
- tourism agencies (government and private);
- individuals within expatriate communities;
- some small and medium enterprises;
- churches with international affiliations;
- physicians, health centres and hospitals;
- communication organizations (newspapers, radio, television); and
- computer and telecommunication companies.

Awareness building initiatives can make use of such existing user groups to provide testimonials, demonstrations and public opportunities to share their experiences with non-users. Groups that are already active in using the Internet in rural and remote areas can provide persuasive information on cost savings, efficiencies and effectiveness, as well as obstacles and solutions to overcoming them. Awareness building initiatives must also travel to the potential user's location, and demonstrate Internet tools within the context in which they may be adopted.

8

Internet and the Future of Communications

The growth of the Internet is a worldwide phenomenon. From a relatively obscure academic tool, the Internet has become a household fixture and nowadays it is hard to find anyone without an e-mail address or a personal home page. As more and more people are becoming wired, the Internet itself is fast becoming as pervasive as televisions and radios. However, its ability to generate many-to-many communication sets it apart from these traditional mass media.

Internet is a strong potential in forming communities, and where there are communities, there are cultures unique to each community. The potential of the Internet in forming "virtual" communities incurs a number of problems, chief among which is the relation between the community formed by the Internet itself and the existing communities bound by locality and cultural tradition. The Internet at the moment is still predominantly American, but it is increasingly global, with more and more countries adding more and more host machines, expanding the network at a breathtaking speed. Network Wizard say that the growth of Internet hosts in 1994 was 15% in Asia alone, and in Thailand the growth rate was as much as 53%. This expansion has created a problem of how local cultures adapt themselves to this novelty.

As a quintessentially Western product, there is clearly bound to be a contrast, if not necessarily a conflict, between non-Western cultures and the Internet technologies. How, in particular, do local cultures take to the Internet and other forms of computer-mediated communication such as the Bulletin Board System (BBS)? Does the Internet represent an all unifying force, turning all cultures within its domain into one giant superculture where everything becomes the same? Does the idea of the Internet and other forms of computer - mediated communication carry with it cultural baggage of the West, such as democracy and individualism?

Thai cultural attitudes do affect computer-mediated communication in a meaningful way. This means the idea that the Internet would automatically bring about social change in line with developments in the West needs to be critically examined. It appears from the study that important presuppositions of local cultures are very much alive, and exist alongside the imported Western ideas. Which type of cultural attitudes and presuppositions is present is more a matter of pragmatic concern, such as whether the participants in CMC happen to find any use for a set of ideas, than that of truth or falsity of the ideas in questions.

Kanchit Malaivongs say that Internet connection in Thailand first took shape in 1988 when an e-mail only dial up account was set up between Prince of Songkhla University in southern Thailand and the Australian Academic and Research Network (AARNET) through the help of the Australian government. A few years later Chulalongkorn University set up the first permanent leased line connection in July 1992, providing services to faculty and students of the university as well as those of some other participating universities.

The cost of connection was shared among the universities, and faculties and students enjoyed free access. Another permanent connection to the Internet backbone was set up by the National Electronics and Computer

Technology Center (NECTEC), a government agency responsible for computer and information technology issues, and more academic organizations joined in. Soon afterwards the government decided to open up access to the general public and dozens of commercial Internet Service Providers (ISPs) sprang up. Today it is estimated that around 131,000 Thais are enjoying access to the Internet.

For the majority of Thai net surfers, soc.culture.thai (SCT) is by far the most popular Usenet newsgroup. It is perhaps the place in cyberspace for discussion on all sorts of aspects on Thailand, and it deals with all aspects of Thai society and culture. Thais form the majority of the nationalities of discussants in the group. The newsgroup derives is tremendous popularity among Thais and Thai watchers from its free wheeling threads of discussion in a culture where some topics may not be discussed publicly.

Furthermore, the group also serves as a place where struggles for political freedom take place. During the May 1992 incident, when soldiers opened fire to the Thai people fighting for constitutional reform, the newsgroup was one of the means of struggle. The whole world was kept informed of what actually happened, and many Thais who were locked out of reliable information due to government blackout of the national media relied on it to learn what was happening outside their homes. Nowadays, when the political climate is much freer, the newsgroup still remains politically active. Members of the newsgroup cherish the freedom to openly discuss forbidden topics with fellow members. Such topics include the personal characters of the members of the royal family, and criticisms, or in many cases, invectives against the politicians.

Since Thais can apparently talk and discuss freely on the Internet without fears of reprisal from the authorities, it is understandable that they would want the same amount of freedom outside of the newsgroup too. What is emerging from many discussion threads in the group is that the participants want to see a new Thailand which is more open and more in tune with the world community — a country that is less bound to the past while still retaining its own cultural identity. The thread started from an important event in recent Thai history, when the King signed the new constitution into law. Discussion then ensued in SCT concerning the new constitution. Naturally the discussants hoped that the new constitution would bring a new era in Thai politics, an era when the old dirty, vote buying, voters bullying, raw power politics would be over.

This is more of an expression of anger than a deliberation. However, the rationale behind it is clear. Sanpawat comments that the next generations of Thais would be more qualified and more responsible than the present one, presumably due to better education and more openness. 'Hea' means 'monitor lizard,' a much lower ranking animal in the Thai cosmos than bovines. While bovines are merely stupid, monitor lizards are treacherous and evil. Bovines are viewed by Thais as beneficial, as they help them with tilling the fields.

Many Thais feel a certain sense of gratitude to them. Monitor lizards, on the other hand, are always keen to steal the farmers' chickens and ducks. The word 'hea' is in Thai a strong invective used to describe those who are bad and depraved. By mixing Thai words in the more or less English posts in SCT, the contributors do not as much aim at being fully understood by the global community than at talking and sharing feelings within his rather close knit community. Here those who don't happen to understand these words and the presupposed background knowledge necessary for grasping the whole meaning, would feel left out. Thus, SCT takes on a double function.

On the one hand, it acts as a channel of disseminating information about Thailand and its people. On the other, it serves as a means by which Thai people and non-Thais who are "in the know" strengthen their shared feelings and knowledge. It is as if the newsgroup is a coffeehouse where people who know one another very well come to discuss things in which they are interested. They don't quite care whether outsiders would be able to follow what is going on. That is not the point of the communication. Such a communication as happening here has its essential function within a community. It is the place where members of the community come to share views, thoughts and feelings, thus making the community itself possible.

This view of communication as the means of strengthening community ties is called by James Carey the 'ritual' view. In Communication as Culture Carey states that there are two views on communication, namely the 'transmission' and the 'ritual' views. The former view communication as a one way traffic, where information, injunctions, news, and the like is 'transmitted' from the source of power to remote posts.

One purpose of such transmission is to create political unity and to assert the power of the political center to areas within its jurisdiction. The ritual view, on the other hand, views communication, not primarily as a means of transmitting information, but as an integral part of community activity, which members of a community perform in order to reaffirm the identity of the community itself. The invectives against the Thai political leaders in the SCT are parts of government bashing occurring after the great flowering of media freedom following the Black May Incident of 1992.

Released from the fear of criticizing the authorities, Thais began to view the government not as somebody from far above, but as one of their own. Once they feel that criticizing the government incurs no real threat to their safety and freedom, Thais are enjoying this freedom a lot, and sometimes it may seem that the criticisms serve merely to release pent up emotions and frustrations rather than to offer constructive viewpoints toward solving the country's problems. What is rather surprising in this phenomenon is that, not only highly educated, middle class Thais are joining in this bashing frenzy, but the poor farmers in the countryside are joining the fray too.

Traditionally these poor farmers, who form the majority bulk of the Thai population, have a very high respect and awe for their rulers, including political leaders and bureaucrats. But they are beginning to feel, in the more democratic and liberal climate, that the leaders are merely humans, and most importantly that they do have real power and leverage against them. Since these leaders do come to power only through their votes, the villagers are getting more involved in politics; they are trying to wrench power to take care of their own affairs from the bureaucrats. A new community is emerging that is bound by the sense of independence and increasing responsibility in dealing with one's own affairs.

Another thread in the newsgroup from which we can see cultural implications concerns the use of language in postings. Kritchai Quanchairat, a regular contributor to the newsgroup, is a Thai computer scientist specializing in localizing certain Internet softwares. He is known for his campaign for more postings in Thai language.

We was under the impression that this n/g was created to discuss and disseminate aspects of the Thai culture, social and political scene. The vast majority of people using this n/g do not read/write Thai so posts in Thai will restrict the original purpose. By all means set up a Thai language n/g. It is a fact that the common language of the internet is English, being either the first or second language of the majority of users. Surely it is a desirable aim that the information on the internet should be accessible to the widest possible audience. To progress academically, socially and economically in Thailand one MUST be competent in the English language. What better incentive could there be for kids who wish to join the on-line community?

Kritchai's attempt to persuade SCT members to use Thai in their posts amounts to nothing less than changing the whole face of the group. However, he has a point. The level of English understanding in the country is generally poor, and the language is not in widespread use at all. Proficient users of the language are few compared to the whole population. Thus, Kritchai apparently believes that if Thai is used more in SCT, more Thais would be persuaded to join and the ensuing discussions would be good for them.

Another reason in favor of using Thai in SCT concerns power relation among different language speakers, as implicitly stated in Kritchai's post. Thais sometimes feel it unfair that they have to communicate in a foreign language instead of their own; they often feel inferior to native English speakers just because their English is not so good as enabling them to talk as fast or to argue as effectively as the natives. Using Thai in this context amounts to an empowering of non-English speakers so they feel confident enough and less self conscious enough to participate actively in the newsgroup. Since English has never gained a foothold in the country except as a foreign language, many Thais feel resistant to the idea of having to talk in English on matters about themselves and their culture. They don't feel that SCT is a forum about Thailand and its culture, but they appear to feel that it is also for Thais and sometimes Thais only. In a tight, close knit culture as the Thai one, such feelings are not uncommon.

Internet as Globalizing Agent

Does the Internet succeed in turning all cultures of the world into one monolithic culture where all the important beliefs and background assumptions are the same? In one sense, it would appear so. When participants of widely disparate cultures come to interact, what happens is that there emerge a kind of culture which is devoid of historical backgrounds that give each local culture its separate identity; it is, the culture of international conferences.

The newly emerging culture is comparable to piped music one hears in airports or in modern supermarkets; that is, it is shorn of its value, its role in a people's scheme of things. It plays no part in the ritual of a traditional culture. In short, it has become sanitized and modernized. Let us call this kind of culture the 'cosmopolitan' one.

One aspect of the Internet clearly points to that kind of culture. When people from all parts of the globe communicate with one another, it is difficult enough when they face each other to observe all the non verbal cues. But since the Internet communication happens almost exclusively through texts, the task becomes much more difficult. Communication requires that participants share at least some sets of values and assumptions together. They have to accept that what others say is largely true some argues. Thus these sets of values and assumptions already exist in a text-mediated community, even though texts are the only means of communication, of building and maintaining the community. These values, however, do not belong to any local, traditional culture, but are whatever that make global computer-mediated communication possible.

It is well known that the shared set of values and assumptions prevalent on the Internet resembles that of liberalism and egalitarianism typical of modern Western liberal culture. The origin of the Internet as a repository for exchanges of discussion and information by computer scientists and other scholars point to the fact that the Internet bears the stamp of the culture of this group. Its birthplace in the United States explains why these assumptions and values are so well embedded.

Nonetheless, the potential of the Internet as the global forum of international communication makes it almost necessary that this shared set of values and assumptions is held by the participants. The set is an outcome of an international, cosmopolitan culture where participants share little in common in terms of historical backgrounds. In order to make communication possible among those who come from disparate historical, traditional backgrounds, the values and assumptions germane to a particular local culture cannot do the job. What happens is that the participants either talk about their professional matters, the topic of international conferences, or they talk about superficial stuffs that guarantee to be shared already, like the weather.

The Internet does not have to originate in the United States for it to acquire the cultural traits it already has. It could have come from Japan, but when it is truly globalized it has no choice but to be what it is now. It is in this sense, then, that the Internet could be regarded as a globalizing agent. This shared set of values and assumptions typical of the Internet becomes apparent when it spreads its roots to states where the ideas of liberalism, egalitarianism, and democracy face violent resistance from the political authorities. The newsgroup soc.culture.burma, for example, is used by Burmese dissidents living abroad to spread information which would not be known otherwise. It is no surprise that the Burmese government even requires its citizens to ask for official permission to own a modem. Failure to do so can make one a political prisoner. That is what happens when governments actively attempt to stop the wishes of its people, and it shows how potent the Internet can be as a political force. It also shows that, if we take the ideas of democracy and respect for human rights as universal, then the Internet could be seen as a harbinger of these ideals to the areas where the ideals are not appreciated by the authorities.

This aspect of the Internet as a harbinger of the liberal ideals could be taken to substantiate the claim that the Internet represents a global force spreading Western values to the world, as if it were the destiny of the world to subscribe fully to Western ideals. However, a distinction should have to be made between Western culture and cosmopolitan culture. Western culture is a product of more than two thousand years of continuously evolving civilization. It has its own traditions, customs, belief systems, religions, which put it on a par with the world's other great civilizations, such as Indian or Chinese.

Cosmopolitan culture, on the other hand, is borne out of the need for people from different cultures to communicate or to do other things with one another. Thus it is by nature shorn of any resources that could be drawn from centuries of experiences. What is happening with the Internet is perhaps not a spread of the former, but the latter. But that is hardly surprising. It is true that cosmopolitan culture originated first in the West, because the need for finding common ground among people of disparate beliefs was first felt there; that, however, does not mean that the two cultures are one and the same.

Thus, when the Internet is used as a political tool, it does not necessarily mean that it acts as a Westernizing force. The majority of SCT contributors who criticize the Thai government are Thais, and here the newsgroup could have been a traditional Thai coffeehouse where people gather and talk and discuss politics. The participants in the newsgroup do not become less Thai when they surf in cyberspace. Instead as they become more active in the affairs of their country, they show that they are more attached to their locales.

Moreover, as the Thai participants can use, and have indeed used, the Internet to spread information on various aspects of the traditional culture, such as traditional recipes and digitized traditional music and paintings, the Internet can even be a tool for cultural preservation and propagation. In this sense it does not globalize, but localize, making people more attuned to their own cultural heritage. Nonetheless, as an embodiment of cosmopolitan culture, it is clear that the Internet globalizes in this way—as a means by which global communication and community building, if only "thinly" in Michael Walzer's sense, becomes possible.

According to Walzer, moral arguments are "thin" when they are shorn of their particular histories and other cultural embodiments which make them integral parts of a cultural entity. These are the parts that make the arguments "thick." To use Walzer's own example, when Americans watched Czechs carry placards bearing words like 'Truth' and 'Justice,' they could relate immediately to the situation and sympathized with the marchers. However, when the arguments are at the local level, as to which version of distributive justice should be in place, there might well be disagreements, and Americans may find themselves disagreeing with the particular conception of justice which is eventually adopted. The sympathetic feeling one feels across the Ocean is part of the "thin" morality, but the localized and contextualized working of those moral concepts is part of the "thick".

The thread of discussion in SCT concerning the language to be used in the forum illustrates the tension between local and global cultures, or thick and thin conceptions, very well. As usually happens in international conferences, talking only about the weather to those with whom one does not share much is rather boring. Many non-Thai Internet surfers do not know much about Thailand and the variously subtle nuances of her culture; thus their contributions are generally limited to asking for information, and when they venture to provide information or ideas of their own, they often reveal that they are quite ignorant of the deeply rooted culture.

In order to communicate with non-Thais on topics related to Thai culture, Thais have to supply an adequate amount of background information in order to make themselves understood. It is much easier for them just to talk to fellow Thais who already share such background knowledge. This way they can mix Thai words in the posts, refer to 'kwais' or 'heas,' or allude to characters in the classical literature without fear of not being understood. Consequently, participants in international gatherings sometimes drift off to form their own smaller groups, banding with those to whom they share background knowledge. The situation also happens on the Internet.

The founding charter of SCT states that the newsgroup is created in order to exchange information and viewpoints about Thailand and its culture, and that English is to be the only medium of communication. But since most Thais do not use English very well, the campaign to post in Thai language is understandable. There also has been an attempt to amend the SCT charter to make it officially recognized to post in Thai. The implication this debate has for the question whether the Internet is a globalizing force is clear.

The ongoing debate in SCT on what language is to be used, together with the defacto existence of a significant portion of SCT posts which are entirely in the Thai language, provide an evidence that, instead of looking at the Internet as a sign of the world becoming culturally monolithic, we may have to look at it just as a global forum where participants join one another so long as there is a felt need for it. And when they feel more comfortable talking to someone back home, so to speak, they don't feel any qualms in forming smaller groups within the big gathering, where they can forget the learned lingua franca and enjoy talking in the vernacular.

To assume that the Internet would bring about a culturally monolithic world would mean that it would bring about a set of shared assumptions and values, including respect for human rights, individualism, egalitarianism, in other words the ideas of contemporary liberal democratic culture. But since it is conceivable that those liberal ideals could exist within cultures other than those of the West, to claim that the Internet would bring about the same "thick" culture in Walzer's sense would seem to be mistaken.

If the set of ideals is viewed instead as a part of the cosmopolitan culture, then it appears that the set will be adopted by a local culture if it feels that it wants or needs to be a part of the global community. And if they don't feel the need, then they will just turn their back on it, in effect telling the world that they don't care to join. Very often in those cases the wish of the populace runs counter to that of the political leaders; political oppression and prohibition of freedom of expression result.

If the culture believed to be "exported" by the Internet is viewed as a cosmopolitan one, and not the traditional Western culture, then we are in a good position to assess the claim that the Internet is a homogenizing cultural force. Since cosmopolitan culture is neutral on most respects, the claim that the Internet will bring it about is rather trivial.

On the other hand, if traditional, or Walzer's "thick," culture is at issue, then it seems the Internet fails to provide such a culture. But now the crucial question is: To which culture do the salient aspects of modern liberal culture, namely respect for human rights, democracy, egalitarianism, belong? Or do they belong to secular, cosmopolitan culture, the culture arising out of the need of people from various cultures to get in touch with one another? To answer this question deeply enough and satisfactorily enough would itself require at least another paper. But at least a glimpse of the way toward an answer can here be given. We have seen from the examination above of what happens in SCT that it is certainly possible for Thais to fight for democracy and human rights, while retaining their distinct cultural identities.

The invectives against the government are just some indications of the concerns of the Thai people on their government and their own country; behind an invective lies a vision of how the country should be governed, a vision that does not include the current political leaders.

On the other hand, the debate on the language to be used in the newsgroup shows that Thais are conscious of their identities and the need to form their own smaller communities within the globalized cyberspace. That the threads happen together in the same newsgroup show that Thais do not view the struggle for more openness, more efficient government, more participatory democracy and so on as something separated or incompatible from the desire to assert their cultural identity. There is no necessary conflict between these two spheres of culture, in the same way as there is no necessary conflict between Bach's chorales and the Gothic buildings on the one hand, and the democratic, libertarian, and egalitarian ideals on the other.

Thai attitudes toward the CMC technologies, especially the Internet, seem to show that the technologies only serve as a means that makes communication possible, communication which would take place anyway in some other form if not on the Internet. Most Thais welcome the new technologies, thinking that they enable them to surge forward with the world. However, this is a far cry from claiming that the Internet would bring about a culturally monolithic world where everybody shares the same "thick" backgrounds and values. What is there in the SCT newsgroup is that Thai people and non-Thais who want to join talk about matters that are interesting to them, be they politics, or culture, or whatever. Here the newsgroup act more like the traditional Thai coffeehouse where public matters, especially local and national politics, dominate the discussion.

As the Internet is really a form of the media, and in Thailand it has been heavily promoted that way, it is an open to the world at large, where, to paraphrase Marshall MacLuhan, one can extend one's senses far from what is normally possible. One can perceive what is going on in far corners of the world in an instant, and especially in the case of the Internet, one can feel as though one is bodily transported to the remote regions one is interacting with.

What comes naturally from such a scenario is that there are bound to be comparisons from what one perceives in the far corners and in the local areas around oneself. When one sees in the far corners what one believes to be good for one's own locality, it is natural to suppose that there are going to be changes in the latter. Rorty's argues that the process is what actually lies behind the universalist rhetoric claiming for a common morality and social norms for all mankind. This process of changes in one's locality as a result of one's perception of other regions, according to Rorty, should not be taken to imply that there is a universal ethics at work. Rorty's naturalism would make such an ethics redundant. What is really the case is that some people just want to live like others. Thus instead of a universal consciousness that this is the right way to live, Rorty claims that there is "solidarity" for mankind.

Hence, when a Thai Internet surfer sees what is going on in another region of the globe which she sees should be good for her own country, be it the strict enforcement of the law, open democracy, human rights and so on, the feelings are those of wanting to be a part of the community that she finds acceptable. Deciding freely on her own, there is then no need that her own cultural identity needs to change. She can remain Thai while embracing all these political and social ideals. That is to say, she can enjoy Thai food and Thai music while struggling for a more open democracy in Thailand at the same time.

Thus the Internet and local cultures both determine each other. While the Internet is a window to the world where influences can be received, the content of the Internet is obviously determined by whatever posted or uploaded to interconnected computers. The information available shows that cultural groups are as separated from one another as they are in the outside world. The cultural fault lines, so to speak, stay roughly the same. An outsider would feel as much lost in the cyberspace of SCT as they could be when dropped in the midst of a Thai town.

Hence communication in SCT could be seen as part of the rituals that make up the Thai identity. The identity, however, is not something static, but is constantly evolving so as to respond effectively to outside changes. Thus there is no contradiction in saying that the Thai identity, for example, evolves in such a way that the Thai people accepts ideals such as human rights, democracy, and the like as their own, as integral parts of their culture. Cyberspace mirrors real space, and vice versa.

Internet and the Forces of Massification

The Internet is finally passing through the period of hype and unrealistic expectations that always accompanies the introduction of a new communications technology. The rhetoric during this early stage typically embraces the technology's revolutionary potential. Forecasters often proclaim that the new technology "will overcome historical forces and political obstacles that prevented previous utopias". In the case of the Internet, its most frequently discussed "revolutionary" characteristics are its ability to foster communication within small, specialized interest groups; to provide greater choice and flexibility in content consumption; and to move us further away from the mass society paradigm.

The Internet frequently has been hailed as a release from the restrictions imposed by the conventional one-to-many format of existing mass media. Though the Internet certainly has begun to realize some of this revolutionary potential, these forecasts typically fail to account for the behavioral, economic, and institutional forces that can constrain a new technology within existing parameters. A number of these forces are working to maintain the mass audience paradigm within the Internet environment. These forces need to be considered when forecasting the future of the Internet.

Characteristics of a Mass Medium

Before addressing these issues, it is important to discuss what is meant by a "mass" medium. Precise and stable definitions of the term are difficult in an era of rapidly evolving media technologies; however, some fundamental components need to be established. An early definition of mass communication included the following characteristics: (a) It is directed toward large, heterogeneous, and anonymous audiences; (b) Messages are transmitted publicly, often timed to reach most audience members simultaneously; and (c) The communicator tends to be, or operate within, a complex organization that may involve great expense. A mass medium would be categorized as any medium containing these three characteristics.

This is due to the potential for new media technologies to essentially eliminate the process of mass communication as it has been traditionally defined. The potential abolition of the term "mass communication" has even been the topic of academic panel discussions. However, in contrast to those who claim that the term has lost its utility, some argue that the concept of mass media remains useful, even in the age of "narrowcast" media. They argue that the simultaneous delivery component of the traditional definition is not inherent in the mass audience/mass media concept.

Mass audiences can be aggregated over time or across various media through "windowing". Webster and Phalen also comments that the undifferentiated audience concept is more ideal-typical than it is a valid representation of mass media audiences through the years, since practitioners have always recognized the possibility that mass audiences could be differentiated.

The analysis will retain within the definition of mass communication the centrality of the institutional communicator. It will also retain the idea that the communicator is fundamentally concerned with some degree of audience maximization, whether it is a specialized channel attempting to maximize its audience of golf aficionados or a broadcast network concerned primarily with gross ratings points.

In addition, the working definition for this analysis will also retain, though to a lesser degree, the traditional definition's emphasis on media content having a relatively broad appeal. The analysis argues that forces affecting the development of the Internet will make the institutional production and distribution of content—with the intention of maximizing particular audiences—and the widespread consumption of mass appeal content, central characteristics of this emerging medium.

Audience Behavior

Researchers have long recognized a certain degree of audience passivity in media consumption. This observation has been used to explain in part the shift in media consumption from print to broadcast media. It has also been used to explain the failure of many forms of "demanding" or interactive media content or services. Some argues that this passive tendency is a preserving force for traditional mass media: "People are passive and only partially attentive to what they see and hear from the media. . . . Searching through obscure and unpopular titles and genres is the obsession of a tiny avant-garde elite, not the great bulk of the populace". To what degree are these conclusions, which were primarily derived from new cable technologies, transferable to the Internet? Given that cable technology has similar interactive, high-bandwidth, and channel diversity capabilities that are said to distinguish the Internet from existing media, we should expect these findings to have substantial relevance.

As evidence, consider the recent emphasis Internet service providers have placed on "push" technology. Push technology automates the delivery of content, thereby "blurring the distinction between the Internet and broadcast media like television". Many within the Internet services industry consider the current manual search model unsustainable over the long term. According to one industry source, "People want their computers to be as easy as their television. . . . They want just a few channels that they can turn to".

Whether or not this assessment is entirely accurate, it is still affecting content and service decisions. This evolutionary regression away from interactive searching and toward passive reception is largely a response to limitations in how audiences will consume media content. Audiences consuming "just a few channels" certainly suggests the presence of the mass audience paradigm within the Internet.

Passive audience consumption tendencies also favor the institutional communicator. The institutional communicator provides valuable gatekeeping services as content provider, selector, and scheduler. Once the institutional communicator is placed in this position of prominence, the provision and consumption of broad appeal content is much more likely, given the economic realities of the media content industry and the nature of audience preferences.

Evolution of Media Use

Neuman's point regarding the "avant-garde elite" component of the audience brings us to the issue of the demographic characteristics of Internet users and how they are likely to change as diffusion levels increase. Recent statistics indicate that 23 percent of people over the age of 16 are using the Internet. These users tend to have higher than average levels of income and education. Given that less than a quarter of the population uses the Internet, and given the characteristics of this group, we can safely say that the Internet is reaching the end of the "elite" stage of the three-stage process of media evolution.

As a new medium moves into the second stage—the "popular stage"—it becomes accessible to the masses, and content shifts in order to appeal to a larger segment of the population. Consequently, as the Internet moves from an elite to a popular medium, there will be an inevitable shift as content changes in order to appeal to a less sophisticated audience. Thus, increased Internet penetration itself becomes a force of "massification." Recent demographic shifts in Internet users indicate that the Internet is becoming more "mainstream" in its demographic make-up. This trend should continue as the Internet moves toward critical mass as a commercial medium.

In order to facilitate broader appeal, Internet content providers will need to alter their content. In fact, many content providers have recently begun to do this. Their strategy involves duplicating the television viewing experience as closely as possible. Internet content providers are turning to such television-based mass appeal formats as talk shows, comedy programs, soap operas, and science fiction series in order to boost subscribership.

America Online recently announced a complete overhaul of its format in an effort to attract another two to three million subscribers. This overhaul involves establishing "channels" based on subjects of interest, as well as daily content changes revolving around television-style programming categories such as "good morning," "prime time," and "late night". According to one industry analyst, "The company has to go after the real mass- market, couch-potato crowd... So [AOL CEO] Pittman is making America Online more like a TV network". Such a strategy certainly makes sense given the preliminary indications that new World Wide Web users are likely to conceive of the Web within the context of traditional mass media, such as the newspaper and television.

It is important to note that this new audience segment is less sophisticated not only in terms of its content tastes, but also in terms of computer literacy. This too works as a force of "massification." Personal computers have still only penetrated about 40 percent of U.S. households. For Internet use to truly explode, this percentage must increase substantially, or, at the very least, users will require a less complex, less expensive tool for accessing the Internet.

The introduction of WebTV is just such a development, and its introduction provides an indication of the degree to which the Internet may need to be integrated into the traditional mass media in order to achieve high levels of penetration. Recently, Microsoft, as well as a number of competitors, have announced the introduction of "second generation" WebTV technology.

This technology provides access to the television and the Internet simultaneously. This new development allows the user to "watch a TV show and be alerted if the programmer has prepared special Web pages that offer more information about the show". With this approach, the Internet literally becomes supplementary to traditional television. If this is indeed the process by which the masses will integrate the Internet into their existing media use, then we can certainly expect the Internet to follow historical precedent and bear a very close resemblance to traditional mass media in terms of the type of content consumed by the audience.

The issue of critical mass mentioned above is another force compelling the Internet to function as a mass medium. Critical mass refers to the point in a new technology's diffusion at which adoption becomes self-sustaining. However, for communications technologies, achieving this critical mass often depends heavily upon users receiving "network externalities" from the new technology. Thus, purchasing a video telephone becomes increasingly appealing as the number of other video telephone users increases. If few other people own a video telephone, then purchasing one makes less sense.

This dependence upon others is a force that can work against the adoption of new technologies. Markus (1987) argues that there are enormous difficulties in attracting users to an interactive medium, due to the degree to which its value lies in its network externalities. Consequently, "interactive media are extremely vulnerable to start-up problems and discontinuance". This situation helps explain why the telephone diffused at a slower rate than radio, television, cable, pay TV, or the VCR.

The appeal of these mass communication technologies depended less upon their network externalities. The diffusion of radio didn't skyrocket until Westinghouse Vice President Harry P. Davis realized the medium's potential for mass communication and began broadcasting concerts from a newly upgraded transmitting station. This conception of radio as more than a point-to-point medium was essential to its rapid growth. The fact that the one-to-many structure promotes faster diffusion than the purely interactive structure has important implications for the future of the Internet. Specifically, a traditional mass communication model is more likely to attract new users. As a result, the one-to-many structure characteristic of mass communication will remain a viable and appealing model within the Internet environment.

Economic Approach to Audience Behavior

The economic approach to audience behavior also provides important insights into the future form and content of the Internet. In general, higher production budgets for media content generate larger audiences. This has been demonstrated as a rational explanation for audience behavior in terms of the consumption of a variety of media products, including films, television programs, and newspapers.

The implications of this phenomenon for the Internet should be clear. First, minority appeal content is always at a competitive disadvantage versus mass appeal content due to its necessarily smaller production budget. Also, institutional producers of media content generally have greater financial resources than individuals and can therefore produce content with larger budgets. Consequently, the institutional communicator that is central to working definition of mass media is likely to dominate a substantial portion of audience attention on the Internet.

Media Economics

This economic approach to audience behavior leads naturally into the second major factor compelling a mass media orientation for the Internet—the economics of the production of media content. Media products are "public goods"; that is, a media product is not used up in consumption. The fact that one audience member watches a television program or visits a Web site does not reduce what is available to other audience members.

In some instances, it is necessary to package the public good in a private good to facilitate distribution. However, the content within the private good remains a public good. Thus, media content production typically involves large, fixed "first copy" costs. In this situation, any audience member willing to pay a non-zero amount for the product contributes to profits. This fact, combined with the fact that audience members' valuations of a media product differ, has given rise to the phenomenon of "windowing," in which the same content is distributed sequentially through various media on the basis of the audience's willingness to pay.

These fundamental characteristics of media economics provide a strong imperative to maximize audiences, thereby achieving economies of scale and distributing the fixed costs over the largest possible audience. These attributes are perfectly translatable to the Internet, where the bulk of the costs are fixed. In addition, Internet users certainly do not use up the content of a Web site or bulletin board in consumption, making Internet content very much a public good. Consequently, the economies of scale in maximizing audience size are also present.

Thus the Internet meets all of the economics of production criteria that have traditionally compelled previous generations of media technologies to function primarily as mass media. Evidence that the same economic forces are at work can be seen in America Online's decision to pattern its business strategy after those of the broadcast networks and the cable industry. Specifically, AOL is attempting to become both producer and distributor of entertainment content. It is also trying to broaden the distribution of its properties beyond the Internet, essentially "windowing" its Internet content through other media technologies.

In a parallel development, start- up companies have begun licensing Hollywood films for distribution on-line. Clearly, just as recent new media technologies such as cable, videocassette recorders, and pay-per-view systems have become important windows for mass appeal content, so too should we expect the Internet to fit into a niche in the windowing sequence.

Consider also the question of risk. Entering the media content production business is inherently risky, and is even more so when producing content for a new media technology whose long-term viability has yet to be determined. Given the high fixed costs of media content production, the producer risks substantial losses if his or her product is rejected by the audience. In an effort to mitigate this risk factor, Hollywood studios produce sequels, remakes, and adaptations of popular books and television programs. This is also why many television series are derived from motion pictures.

Audience familiarity with content already proven popular acts as a risk reducer. As profit-oriented firms move into the production of Internet content, they will logically behave in a similar manner, relying heavily on content that has demonstrated appeal in order to reduce risk. Thus, we can expect Internet content not only to duplicate content from existing mass media, but to duplicate that content which has had the greatest popular appeal, thereby further reducing the risk involved.

Another important economic consideration is that there will always remain a certain degree of advertiser demand for mass audiences. According to Turow, mass audiences will continue to be desirable for two reasons: (a) to reach consumers who would never be expected to buy the product (thereby enhancing the product's "badge value" for those who can afford it); and (b) because broad campaigns signal that products have wide appeal.

Advertiser desire for large audiences has been a maintaining factor for mass appeal television. Witness, for instance, the discussion surrounding the enormous contracts that NFL football signed with a number of broadcast networks and cable stations. Though audience numbers have declined in recent years, prices skyrocketed, since professional sports remains one of the few program types that can still generate enormous and extremely heterogeneous mass audiences. Obviously, the increasing scarcity of such mass audiences has placed a premium on them. We should expect this phenomenon to transfer to the Internet as well, thus motivating content providers to assemble mass audiences.

Finally, it is important to consider the role of institutional forces in the development of new media technologies and the implications for the Internet's prospects as a mass medium. The forms that new technologies take, as well as their impacts on society, are integrally related to the dynamics of social and organizational structures".

Influx of Existing Media Organizations

Commercial media organizations are actively moving into the Internet. A 1995 search found 123 different U.S. newspaper services and more than 1,300 magazine services with distinct Web sites. In addition, over 200 television stations have Web pages, as do a number of cable networks, production companies, and the broadcast networks. Mammoth organizations such as AT&T, Microsoft, and NBC have invested substantial sums in the provision of Internet content. Recently, Disney initiated efforts to purchase Starwave, a large World Wide Web content provider.

This influx of existing media organizations into a new media technology follows historical precedent. Some says, "The same authorities and institutions, the same capital, the same effort which created today's world is trying also to create tomorrow's". As a result, the new system becomes established in the image of the old system and becomes part of the existing institutional structure. Thus it is not surprising that the motion picture studios dominate the videocassette industry, that the radio networks became the major forces in television, and that the broadcast networks have substantial ownership in cable channels. As this pattern continues with the Internet, we will again see the predominance of institutionally produced content that is fundamental to the traditional definition of mass media.

In addition, given that we are witnessing the movement into this new technology of content producers who traditionally have engaged in the production of mass appeal content, and that these large organizations need to exploit the economic principles of media production discussed above in order to remain viable and maximize profits, we may reasonably expect the content they produce for the Internet to be designed to appeal to mass audiences. Corporations generally view new technologies in terms of integrating them into the existing "system". The development of television content was characterized by the migration of radio programs and performers to the new medium. Similarly, the videocassette industry is dominated by Hollywood motion pictures, and cable programming generally bears a strong resemblance to traditional broadcast network programming.

Thus, regardless of the niche-appeal potential of a new medium such as the Internet, the established media organizations that move into the new medium "hold a vested interest in carrying people and ideas across various media forms and maintaining the 'mass ritual'".

Early indications substantiate this perspective in terms of the Internet, as on-line magazines have tended to re-publish print material, the motion picture studios have used their web sites primarily to promote current film releases, and television stations have primarily recycled their news broadcasts. Similarly, NBC has begun "intercasting" the Tonight Show in an effort to broaden the program's audience. Thus, both the increasing prevalence of institutional communicators within the realm of the Internet, and the propensity of these communicators to rely on traditional mass appeal content, push the Internet in the direction of a mass medium.

Audience Measurement

The process of commercial media organizations moving into a new medium is always accompanied by the development of audience measurement technologies. Currently, the process of measuring Internet audiences is fraught with technological challenges, including ambiguity about what a "hit" actually means and difficulties in determining the demographic characteristics of Web site visitors. These difficulties, along with the absence of an agreed- upon measurement system, have made large advertisers hesitant to invest heavily in Internet advertising. The development of an audience measurement system that is perceived as reliable is therefore essential to the Internet's long-term commercial viability.

The development of such a system has important implications for the Internet's future as a mass medium. The accuracy with which a media audience can be measured affects the value of that audience. Given that advertisers buy a prospective audience, they are willing to pay a premium for an audience whose actual size is more likely to resemble its predicted size. In addition, advertisers also value the quality (i.e. reliability) of ratings data.

This is relevant to discussion of the Internet's mass media prospects because the accuracy and reliability of audience measurement data increases with the size of the audience. Narrowcast media traditionally have been poorly served by commercial audience measurement companies.

Cable channels with small viewerships have long criticized Nielsen for inaccurately measuring their audiences. Television stations in small markets have been similarly unhappy. Consequently, the process of quantifying Internet audiences will, at least initially, benefit those content providers courting a larger audience, and increase their competitive advantage relative to niche appeal providers.

This competitive advantage increases given the nature of how Internet audiences are measured. Currently, the CPM model dominates Internet advertising transactions. Advertisers purchase a desired quantity of audience members, who are measured only in terms of exposure.

The refinement and improvement of audience measurement techniques can eventually increase the viability of niche media once the measurement techniques and technology have reached a certain level of sophistication. However, at this early stage in the development of Internet audience measurement technology, mass appeal content providers will hold a distinct advantage. Perhaps it is not surprising, then, that at this point two-thirds of all advertising revenues go to the ten most popular advertiser supported Web sites.

Government Response to New Media

It is also essential to consider the government's role in the development of new media technologies. The development of new technologies is inextricably intertwined with the political process. Government regulators and legislators consistently interpret new media technologies within the context of older media technologies. Some states, "judges and legislators have tried to fit technological innovations under conventional legal concepts".

The legal system's foundation on stare decisis shoehorns new technologies into preexisting models and conceptions. According to Mosco the Federal Communications Commission applies a simplifying structure to new technological developments, causing them to respond to new media technologies within the frameworks established by older media technologies. Consequently, some of the innovative potential of these new technologies goes unrealized. Can we expect the Internet to be interpreted by policy makers within the context of traditional mass media? Mueller (in press) demonstrates how the ongoing controversy over the assignment of Internet domain names parallels the initial controversy surrounding the distribution of radio frequencies.

Once again issues of scarcity and property rights predominate, which, according to Mueller, will prompt a new system of Internet governance, just as these issues prompted government regulation of broadcasting. The strength of this historical parallel between the Internet and broadcasting increases the likelihood of the new technology being regulated in a similar manner to the old.

The initial passage of the Communications Decency Act, which installed a distinctly broadcasting-based regulatory framework on the Internet, provides evidence that this tendency exists among policy makers. The Act's concern with the pervasive nature of adult content and children's ease of access are concepts distinctly related to the mass audience framework; specifically, the "audience as victim" approach that has dominated FCC regulation of broadcasting. It should also be noted that, regardless of the outcome of the decision, the Supreme Court's assessment of the Act relied heavily upon seeking analogies to older media technologies.

Thus, historical evidence as well as recent actions suggest that policy making institutions are likely to interpret the Internet within the context of existing mass media. Consequently, they are likely to bias the development and evolution of the Internet in the direction of a mass medium.

This chapter has outlined a number of forces that, when taken together, compel the Internet toward functioning as a mass medium. This discussion has shown that institutional communicators will establish and maintain a significant presence on the Internet, and that economic and audience factors compel the production and consumption of mass appeal content. Potent behavioral, economic, and institutional forces work against the mass audience paradigm as well. These forces have been extensively analyzed elsewhere. Individuals' Internet use habits could provide important insights in this regard. It is also important to determine the degree to which audiences are taking advantage of the Internet's unique capacity by consuming a diversity of content. Methods for assessing "exposure diversity" within traditional mass media could be adapted to similar assessments within the Internet environment.

A statement frequently heard among television executives and academics these days is that "the future of television is radio," suggesting that television channels will more closely resemble the format-specific organization of radio stations in the years to come. This is certainly already happening, with many cable channels providing a single, specific type of programming, much as radio stations devote themselves only to classical music, or only to sports. When assessing the future of the Internet, we can draw a similar analogy. The forces outlined here, along with the preliminary evidence presented, suggest that, to some degree, the future of the Internet is television. The mass audience paradigm has withstood the introduction of cable, the VCR, and satellite. It will endure and flourish on the Internet as well.

Bibliography

Auhja, M. & Carley, K. "Network structure in virtual organizations". *Journal of Computer Mediated Communication*, 1998.

Barker, C. & Groenne, P., *Advertising on the World Wide Web*, 1997.

Berthon, P., Pitt, L. F. & Watson, R. T., The world wide web as an advertising medium: Toward an understanding of conversion efficiency. Journal of Advertising Research, 36(1), 43-54.

Burgess, M. & Mathis, L., "Scenarios for computers in composition". *CMC Magazine* 1996.

Cornwell, R, "Culture of the net", *Internet World*, 1998.

Crede, A., "Electronic commerce and the banking industry: The requirement and opportunities for new payment systems using the Internet". *Journal of Computer Mediated Communication* , 1999.

Cronin, M. J. *Global advantage on the Internet: From corporate connectivity to international connectiveness*. John Wiley & Sons, 1995.

Gunkle, D. J., "Virtually transcendent: Cyberculture and the body". *Journal of Mass Media Ethics*, 13(2), 111-123.

Katz, J. E. & Aspden, P., "Internet dropouts in the U.S.A.: the invisible group. Telecommunications Policy, 22(4/5), 327-339, 1998.

MacLean, Eleanor. *Between the Lines: How To Detect Bias and Propaganda in the News and Everyday Life*. Montreal: Black Rose Books, 1981.

Morris, M. & Ogan, C., "The Internet as mass medium". *Journal of Communication,* 46(1), 39-50, 1996.

Lewis, Peter M. and Booth, Jerry. The Invisible Medium: Public. Commercial and Community Radio. London: Macmillan, 1989.

Nelson, Joyce. Sultans of Sleeze: Public Relations and The Media. Toronto: Between The Lines Press, 1989.

Rushkoff, Douglas. *Media Virus: Hidden Agendas in Popular Culture.* New York: Ballantine, 1994.

Schrank, Jeffrey. *Understanding Mass Media* (Third Edition). Toronto: Copp Clark, 1986.

Index